Andrew MacLaren

Office Location
in Urban and
Regional Development

J. B. GODDARD

GW00597166

Theory and Practice in Geography

OXFORD UNIVERSITY PRESS · 1975

Oxford University Press, Ely House, London W. 1

GLASGOW NEW YORK TORONTO MELBOURNE WELLINGTON
CAPE TOWN IBADAN NAIROBI DAR ES SALAAM LUSAKA ADDIS ABABA
DELHI BOMBAY CALCUTTA MADRAS KARACHI LAHORE DACCA
KUALA LUMPUR SINGAPORE HONG KONG TOKYO

ISBN 0 19 874033 6

©Oxford University Press 1975

*All rights reserved. No part of this publication may be reproduced,
stored in a retrieval system, or transmitted, in any form or by any means,
electronic, mechanical, photocopying, recording or otherwise, without
the prior permission of Oxford University Press.*

*This book is sold subject to the condition that it shall not, by way of
trade or otherwise, be lent, re-sold, hired out, or otherwise circulated
without the publisher's prior consent in any form of binding or cover
other than that in which it is published and without a similar condition
including this condition being imposed on the subsequent purchaser.*

Printed in Great Britain
by J. W. Arrowsmith Ltd.,
Bristol

Contents

Introduction

Office Location Research and Public Policy

This book is about the geography of office activities. It briefly outlines recent trends in the location of office employment and describes some of the research that geographers and others have conducted into the factors that lie behind these trends. The book has an important further aim—that is to set this research in the context of a rapidly developing concern on the part of public policy-makers with issues relating to office location. Research has contributed to the public discussion of office location by highlighting the increasing significance of office jobs to the economic and social development of cities and regions. The policies that have emerged from such discussions—like those designed to encourage the decentralization of offices from capital cities—have in turn influenced the nature of further research. For example, considerable attention has been given by some researchers to the nature of the constraints that appear to tie office jobs to the city centre, while other workers have attempted to evaluate the social and economic consequences of decentralization policies. In this way research has contributed to the revision or reformulation of policy while at the same time giving new theoretical insights into the location processes that underpin this aspect of urban and regional development. Studies of office location illustrate, perhaps more than some fields of geographical research, the dialogue between theoretical work and public policy that is necessary in order for research to make a meaningful contribution to urban and regional problems.

Perhaps one of the most significant tasks of research is to draw attention to the emergence of new types of problems. Office activities had already begun to make their presence felt on the urban scene in the late nineteenth century, and although attempts to shape the development of cities and regions were being made in Britain in the 1930s and 1950s, it was not until the 1960s that the importance of office activities were fully appreciated and office location policies formulated. A natural starting-point for the book is therefore a description of the recent growth of office employment in national economies and its changing geographical distribution. Chapters two and three focus on studies which have attempted to increase our theoretical understanding of the factors influencing office location at the inter-urban and intra-urban levels respectively. In the latter case particular attention is focused on the metropolitan city centre where the great bulk of higher-level office employment tends to be concentrated. Chapter four discusses policies of office decentralization that have aimed at reducing this concentration and research that has attempted to evaluate some of the social and economic consequences of decentralization policies. As one of the principal economic consequences of decentralization is the possible loss of personal contacts that are easily maintained in a central location, Chapter five examines in some detail the communications factor in office relocation in both the public and private sectors.

In demonstrating the effect of location on office communication patterns research on office decentralization policy has added to a developing body of theory on the location of non-manufacturing activities to which flows of information rather than materials are central. Chapter six concludes the book by discussing how this theory can be used in practice—by organizations using relocation as a positive tool for achieving certain management objectives and also by public policy-makers wishing to influence such location decisions.

In view of the importance of public policy in shaping office location research, it is not surprising that most of the material on which the book draws is based upon British and Swedish research, two countries which have had active policies of decentralization from their capital cities coupled with a strong tradition of applied geography. Apart from the pioneering work of the Regional Plan Association in New York, very little research on office location can be found in the United States. The evidence gathered by the Regional Plan Association suggests that much can be learned from comparing experience in different geographical and policy contexts. It is hoped that by drawing together some of the European experience this book will stimulate office location studies in North America and elsewhere.

1 The geography of office employment

What is office employment?

We are all familiar with the conventional threefold classification of economic activity into primary (agriculture, forestry, fishing etc.), secondary (manufacturing), and tertiary (service) sectors. But there is an additional and rapidly growing sphere of activity that does not fit neatly into this classification, what the geographer, Jean Gottman, has called the quaternary sector. This sector includes the professions (e.g. solicitors, accountants, management consultants, etc.) and finance (banking and insurance), which all provide non-physical services to the public at large but specifically to the business community. In addition, this fourth sector includes public activities like central and local government, universities, research institutes, and the like.

Office workers constitute a much higher proportion of all workers in the quaternary sector than they do in any other sector. It is in the quaternary sector that most people work in offices, but people also work in offices within other sectors. For example the mining industry employs a large number of people not directly involved in digging minerals out of the ground but rather in their marketing and distribution. Even the so-called 'pure' office sectors like banking and finance include people not involved in administrative or clerical work. So in identifying office employment a conventional sectoral classification tends to break down. An occupational classification is needed which refers not to the product or services of an organization but to the functions or roles of individuals or groups of individuals within the organization.

What then are office occupations? An alternative way of posing the same question is to ask: what job functions are performed in office premises rather than factories, shops, or warehouses? This formulation reveals that there are both functional and physical office concepts.

Functional concepts

1. *Office activity* refers to individual jobs that involve dealing with information, ideas, or knowledge, e.g. information search, storage, and retrieval, and the exchange and generation of ideas.

2. *Office occupations* refer to groups of office activities handling similar types of information in a similar way, e.g. a research and development expert may search out information, a filing clerk may store and retrieve it, while a manager may make a decision on the basis of this information.

3. *Office organizations* are formal groupings of different office occupations, e.g. a Government department, a private firm, or a University

administration. The pattern of formal *and* informal links between various office activities (i.e. what information is communicated to whom) define the structure of the organization.

Physical concepts

1. *Office buildings* are workplaces whose principal use is for office-type activities and which are equipped with information-handling facilities like typewriters, dictating machines, telephone, telex, filing cabinets, calculating machines, and computer terminals.

2. *Office establishments* are physically separate locations where office activities are conducted. Organizations may have all of their office activities in one establishment or these may be divided between a number of establishments. An organization may include establishments whose dominant activities are not office activities (e.g. a production plant), while other establishments may be devoted exclusively to office work (e.g. the head office for a group of companies).

We may therefore measure office activity in terms of employment (classified by both occupation and sector), office buildings (or more specifically floor space devoted to office usage), and office establishment. We will use the location of office employment and office establishments to describe the recent changes in the geographical distribution of office activities. But first we shall briefly look at the growth of office employment in national economies at large.

The growth of office employment

There can be little doubt that office activities have come to occupy a very significant position in advanced economies. While the export of manufactured products is still basic to most countries in the developed world, success in this field depends increasingly on managerial expertise, particularly concerning the development and marketing of an industry's products. These are all office-type activities. At the same time many industries which are entirely office-based such as banking, insurance, and a wide range of professional services make an important contribution to the so-called invisible earnings of many countries.

In this situation it is not surprising that the numbers of people who work in office-type occupations has rapidly increased. According to the preliminary tabulations of the 1971 Census of the U.K. one out of every four persons in employment in Great Britain had an office occupation compared with under one in six in 1951 (25 per cent compared with 15 per cent of the economically active population). The 1950s in particular witnessed the most spectacular growth of office employment. Between 1951 and 1961, while total employment in England and Wales increased by 7 per cent, employment in office occupations increased by no less than 40 per cent. Office workers therefore accounted for three-quarters of the net increase in the total occupied population during this period. Although most office jobs could be found in the service sector (62 per cent of the total in 1961), office employment was not confined to this sector. In fact the net employment increase in the manufacturing sector during the 1950s was entirely in office jobs. In other words, if it had not been for the growth of office occupations, total employment in the manufacturing sector during the 1950s in Britain would have declined.

There is some evidence in the 1971 Census of a slower growth rate of office occupations during the 1960s when the percentage increase was 23 per cent.[†] Comparisons with the 1966 Census suggests that the rate of growth of office occupations slowed down particularly in the second half of the decade, from 12·2 per cent between 1961 and 1966 to 9·9 per cent between 1966 and 1971. In part this reflects a general slowing-down of economic expansion; moreover, increases in office employment in many sectors frequently compensated for a decrease in other occupations. In a time of slow economic growth, however, there is obviously a limit to the extent to which office occupations can be a panacea to more general problems of full employment.

The difference between the 1950s and 1960s is also reflected in changes in the structure of the office workforce. Whereas the bulk of the growth of office employment during the 1960s was in clerical occupations, as the economic climate became more harsh in the late 1960s this growth was cut back in favour of administrative and professional jobs. Between 1966 and 1971 when total employment *decreased* by 2 per cent, clerical occupations continued to grow but by only 5 per cent with 23 per cent for administrative and professional jobs. The continued growth of high-level office employment possibly reflects the need to devote more managerial resources to long-range planning activities in a time of economic hardship.

Not surprisingly these changes have affected individual business sectors differentially. When the figures are disaggregated it is apparent that many sectors registered an absolute decline in clerical employment during the late 1960s—a notable exception being the public sector. While only 6 per cent of the economically active population of Great Britain were employed in public administration and defence in 1966, this sector nevertheless accounted for 54 per cent of the actual increase in clerical jobs between 1966 and 1971—a total of 81 000 jobs. This should be compared, for example, with the loss of nearly 20 000 clerical jobs in the electrical and instrument engineering sectors alone. The public sector also recorded a 38 per cent increase in higher-level (administrative and professional) office employment, but this represented only 14 per cent of the total increase in this type of job. So in spite of repeated attempts to control

† The 1971 Census figures are only a one per cent sample. 1971 was also a time of very high unemployment compared with 1961 so these data must be interpreted with caution.

the growth of Civil Service and Local Government employment this continued to grow inexorably, the bulk of this growth being in the form of relatively low-level office jobs.

While employment in the manufacturing sectors continued to grow in the 1950s, owing principally to the growth of office occupations, it would appear that much of this growth has subsequently been transferred to the service sector as functions previously performed within manufacturing companies have been contracted out. So while total employment in manufacturing industry declined between 1966 and 1971, higher-level office employment in the professional and scientific services increased by 25 per cent. The decline of the manufacturing sector and the continual rise of the service sector are therefore to some extent complementary.

Trends in the regional distribution of office employment

1. *Great Britain*

The growth of office employment has been far from evenly distributed within most countries. Indeed, the growth of office activities has generally underpinned the rapid development of a limited number of prosperous regions. In England and Wales, the expansion of office employment has been a key component in the growth of the South East region. Although the South East is now experiencing a net migration loss of population to other regions (principally through retirement) it did gain 41 000 economically active migrants during the period 1961–6, and, significantly, 37 000 of these migrants were office workers. During this period migration to other regions was not so dominated by office workers. So by 1966 the South East had 47 per cent of all office employment but only 35 per cent of all employment.

The picture up to the 1966 Census was one of increasing regional concentration especially of higher-level office jobs. As is argued in the next chapter, such jobs are essentially urban functions so data should refer to meaningfully defined urban units. One such definition is provided by Metropolitan Economic Labour Areas (M.E.L.A.s) (Hall 1971), basically an employment core and its commuting hinterland. Unfortunately no office employment data are available for such units. However, socioeconomic group data are a useful proxy.

Westaway has analysed changes in the distribution of professional and managerial, administrative, and manual occupations for 111 M.E.L.A.s between 1961 and 1966 (Westaway 1974a). His analysis has revealed that labour markets in the development areas have experienced a negative shift in their share of managerial and professional occupations. Even major cities like Manchester, Leeds, and Glasgow were not receiving the share of the growth of high-level office jobs that their size and position in the urban hierarchy would suggest. Only in the Yorkshire and Humberside and Northern regions was this relative loss of high-level employment compensated for by above-average growth in clerical jobs.

In contrast labour markets in the more prosperous parts of the country which were already in a favourable position in 1961 generally increased their share of both clerical and administrative office jobs in the next five years. London was an exception amongst labour markets in the South East with the number of economically active males in professional and managerial occupations increasing by 21 000 (+4·1 per cent), but the number in clerical occupations *decreasing* by 19 000. This relative decline in clerical employment was mainly confined to central London and was insignificant compared with a net loss of 131 000 in manual occupations.

If we examine trends in the distribution of office establishments this pattern of concentration is even more marked. Westaway has shown that the head offices of the thousand largest companies in the U.K. are predominantly in London, with an almost perfect correlation between firm size and propensity to locate in the capital. For example, 86 of the 100 largest firms have their head office in London compared with 32 of the 100 smallest. This degree of concentration appears to be increasing over time: between 1969 and 1972 the number of head offices located in London rose by 30 while all other large cities recorded losses. Firms with head offices outside London tend to operate in narrow sectors of the economy with production localized in one part of the country.

Looking at corporate organizations as a whole rather than just head office functions we see that more office-type functions than production plants are principally found in the South East. A survey by Parsons of 224 manufacturing corporations in the U.K. has shown that although the South East accounted for only 28 per cent (507) of all operating units of these companies, it contained 74 per cent (51) of group head offices; 48 per cent (15) of central services units (i.e. those functions concerned with administering the corporation at a geographically distinct location from the group head office); 69 per cent (66) of corporate control units (i.e. group head offices plus central services); 42 per cent (86) of divisional head offices; and 48 per cent (41) of research and development units (Parsons 1972). Comprehensive figures collated by Buswell and Lewis (1970) emphasize the importance of the South East region outside London for research and development in both the public and private sector. They show that the South East contains 49 per cent of all such establishments in the country.

So the South East region would appear to be a favourable environment for a range of office activities, not just head office functions. It is unfortunately impossible to assess how many people are employed in different office functions in the private sector. However, some data are available for the public sector. In 1972, 71 per cent of all headquarters staff in the non-industrial Civil Service worked in the South East region (U.K. 1973). These were generally ministerial offices and the supporting policy-making divisions and other divisions servicing the whole of the department in functions of a national character. Not surprisingly Civil Service employment in local offices and other specialist establishments was more widely dispersed, although again the South East region had more than its fair share. So in spite of official awareness of the need to spread the benefits of public sector employment throughout the nation, government office activities appear to be even more attached to the London region than those in the private sector.

2. *United States*

Office employment is also rather unevenly distributed within the spa economy of the United States, although the concentration here is principally in the largest metropolitan areas rather than a single city region like the South East of England. The 24 metropolitan areas with populations of over one million people have 43 per cent of the nation's office jobs, but only 34 per cent of total population. In the manufacturing sector the same cities have 66 per cent of employment in headquarters-type 'central administrative and auxiliary jobs' but only 39 per cent of production jobs (Armstrong and Pushkarev 1972).

Although it does not dominate the American scene to the extent that London dominates the United Kingdom, New York does occupy a distinctive position. Armstrong and Pushkarev's analysis of location trends in American cities has suggested that administrative jobs in the manufacturing sector at least are either decentralizing gently to smaller metropolitan areas in the wake of their production plants, or if they have to be centralized prefer to locate in New York. In fact manufacturing office employment seems to be inversely related to the size of the metropolita area, with the exception of New York. Again excluding New York, there is a close correspondence between the industrial composition of all manufacturing jobs in the metropolitan area and the industrial composit of office employment, but this is often due to one or two large employe (like General Motors with its head office in Detroit). As in Britain, secto that are highly concentrated in particular regions tend to have their head quarters in that region. Data on office establishments confirm these trends. The 21 largest metropolitan areas in the U.S.A. contain 348 head offices of the 500 leading industrial corporations in 1968 and 140 of these were located in New York. The head offices of organizations in th non-manufacturing sector are generally more concentrated. Indeed these service activities appear to have taken over from manufacturing offices a the main component of office growth in most metropolitan areas.

3. *Sweden*

In Sweden the growth of high-level office employment has been heavily concentrated in the three largest cities, Stockholm, Gothenburg, and Malmo. Total employment in the manufacturing, construction, and wholesale sectors grew in these three cities by 4 per cent, 10 per cent, and 8 per cent respectively between 1960 and 1965. The total number of salaried staff in the highest grades increased by 39 per cent, 46 per cent, and 67 per cent respectively in these three cities compared with an average of 31 per cent for the rest of Sweden (Törnqvist 1970). These trends continued in the second half of the 1960s: over the whole decade higher-level office jobs increased by 61 per cent, 65 per cent and 61 per cent in the three cities compared with an average of 44 per cent in the 43 smallest city regions (Engström and Sahlberg 1973). As in Britain, the share of these top jobs held by smaller cities in the southern and northern parts of the country declined relatively and in some cases absolutely. So by 1970 the Stockholm region had 30 per cent of all top-level jobs in the private sector but only 18 per cent of total population. Top-level office employment in the public sector was even more heavily concentrated in Stockholm—58 per cent of the total compared with 29 per cent of all white collar workers in this sector.

The concentration of specialist business service functions in capital cities is well exhibited by Swedish data although the same tendencies are apparent in other countries (EFTA 1973). For example, Stockholm contains 58 per cent of all advertising agencies, 57 per cent of all computer bureaux, and 51 per cent of all management consultants, while less specialized business services like accountancy are more widely dispersed.

Office decentralization

At the inter-regional scale office activities are strongly concentrating into the larger city regions. Initially much of this activity was confined to the city centre or central business district. Increasingly, however, there is evidence of a substantial decentralization of office employment to other locations within the city regions. American experience suggests that this process is going on irrespective of public intervention aimed at encouraging decentralization—which is the situation in Britain. For a selection of 21 metropolitan areas in the U.S.A., Armstrong and Pushkarev report that in 1960 only 40 per cent of all office employment was found in the central business district. This proportion varied considerably between metropolitan areas: generally, the higher the degree of specialization in office activities the greater the degree of concentration in the central business district. The preference for the suburbs appears to be increasing over time, especially in the largest cities.

Conclusion: office employment and the economic and social development of cities and regions

The outstanding conclusion of this description of the changing distribution of office occupations at the national level is the extreme concentration of office jobs in the most prosperous and rapidly growing parts of many countries coupled with local dispersal from the largest cities. These trends have far-reaching implications for the economic and social development of the nation, implications which policies only now are beginning to reflect. It is also a trend which traditional theories of urban and regional development are poorly equipped to handle.

Questions of regional differences in development have traditionally been approached from either an economic or a social point of view. Problems of industrial development and social structure have frequently been treated in isolation. But because office employment can only be adequately defined in occupational terms and since a person's occupation refers simultaneously to the job he does (i.e. his function within an organization) *and* his position in society (i.e. the resources at his command), occupational structure must form a vital bridge between economic and social considerations in regional development.

The changing distribution of office occupations that we have described must have a direct bearing on local labour market conditions in different parts of a country. We have seen that the job structure of peripheral areas is increasingly dominated by clerical and manual occupations. Regional policies designed to boost employment in absolute terms have traditionally been orientated towards the manufacturing sector and have frequently resulted in the establishment of branch plants which provide few managerial job opportunities. Qualified individuals are forced to migrate out of such areas in order to fulfil a career path determined by an educational system increasingly orientated towards the needs of the office sector. Such out-migration contributes towards a downward economic and social spiral with new enterprises being discouraged by the lack of qualified managerial expertise while individuals are discouraged from proceeding with further education by the lack of local job opportunities. On the other hand the continued influx of well-qualified individuals into the labour markets of large cities like London, coupled with the decentralization of manual and clerical jobs, could lead in the long run to an imbalance in the social structure of such cities.

The economic implications for industry of the concentration of high-level office functions could be equally serious. The problems of the development areas are not only those of an outdated industrial structure and physical inaccessibility to markets and suppliers. We have seen that the principal function of persons involved in office activities is the processing and exchange of information. Because most important information is 'locked up' in high-level office functions which are generally located outside the development areas, firms in these areas could have severe problems of access to the know-how that is essential if they are to adapt to changing economic circumstances. So in addition to accessibility measured in terms of direct transportation for materials and finished products, account needs to be taken of the hidden costs of access to information. In the next chapter we examine theories about the location of office activities and their role in regional development process, theories which pay particular attention to information flows.

2 Office location and the urban system

Factors influencing the location of office activities: the basis for theory

Before we can attempt to alleviate many of the problems of regional disparities in job opportunities and economic development that have been outlined, we need a better understanding of their fundamental causes. Although a body of literature on office location is developing this has mainly been concerned with the intra-urban location of head office functions and of independent firms in the quarternary sector (e.g. professional services). Few attempts have been made to set head office location within the over-all spatial structure of the corporate organizations that are now coming to dominate employment in all sectors.

The concepts that are most relevant to this approach will be found in modern organization theory, although few writers in this field have explicitly considered the effect of location on how an organization operates—that is whether it really makes any difference if the head office is in London or in Manchester or anywhere else. Yet location is obviously important. Modern organization theorists stress the open nature of organizational systems and the importance of interaction between the organization and its social and technical environment. In this context the word 'environment' refers to things like the general state of knowledge and climate of opinion related to the organization's activities. The word also has an important geographical meaning because there is some evidence to suggest that office functions in different locations have a different pattern of access to the environment. These patterns of access will be reflected in information flows which can be mapped into geographical space. It is these information flows that ultimately define how the organization operates, particularly how it is able to adapt to changes in the environment—e.g. by developing new products, selecting new suppliers, and so on.

The critical questions for regional development seem to be: what is the relationship between the spatial structure of organizations and growth and change in these organizations? And how do these differences feed through into differences in aggregate regional performances? The second of these questions is particularly fundamental as it stresses the need to connect what is happening at the micro-level to individual organizations with the fortunes of regions as a whole.

The spatial structure of corporate organizations

One way of making the linkage between organizational and regional structure has been suggested by the Swedish geographer, Olof Wärneryd (Wärneryd, 1968). In this three hypothetical organizations with a hierarchical structure are mapped into geographical space (Fig. 2.1). Various

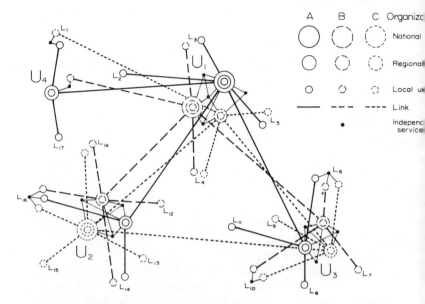

Fig. 2.1. The spatial arrangement and functional character of units within three hypothetical organizations.
U_1 may be thought of as the highest-ranking member of a given system of cities, U_2 as the second-ranking metropolitan area, and U_3 and U_4 as middle-ranking centres of regional importance. L_1–L_{18} are lower-order cities of varying population and local importance.
(from Pred, 1973 after Nordström, 1968)

functions (e.g. group head office, divisional head office, and manufacturing plants) are located at cities in different positions in the urban hierarchy (national capital, regional centre, local centre). Generally the highest-level decision-making functions are performed by units at the top of the organizational hierarchy and these units tend to be located in the largest cities. These offices may also encompass lower-level function which have authority only over parts of the organization and therefore parts of the geographical system over which the organization operates. A complex set of linkages or interdependencies representing these lines of administrative responsibility exists between office establishments in different urban centres. In addition, external linkages exist between organizations—e.g. with service firms in particular cities.

Using this type of model but also stressing interdependence between large cities at the top of the urban hierarchy, Pred has explored the relationship between corporate structure and regional development processes (Pred 1973). In particular he has discussed how the spatial structure of linkages within a company can steer the spread of non-local multiplier effects. Expansion of activities in a branch plant or office, for example, may lead to additional administrative employment at divisional or group head offices rather than locally. If the expansion is in an existing area of business which simply involves more inputs of the same type as previously, the decisions about purchase sources are pre-defined and may be made locally. But when new or specialized inputs are required, this decision is likely to be made at a higher level within the organization and therefore may not ncessarily involve local sources. For example, specialist consultancy services required in connection with a new project may be purchased by the head office from its own local environment rather than by the branch office. So the distribution of office functions within an organization can be a basic cause of one of the well-known problems of industrial development in peripheral areas—i.e. the problem of multiplier leakage back to the congested regions. At the same time small organizations not represented in the capital may have difficulties in obtaining service linkages.

A number of behavioural studies of service linkages have coroborated the significance of this particular perspective on organizational structure and regional development processes. Britton (1974), for example, has examined the supply of office services (e.g. banking and finance, legal services, accountancy, etc.) in contrasting regions of Canada for both single-plant firms and multi-plant corporations. In the case of branches, higher-order services are generally provided by the head office directly or from service firms located near to the head office. Lower-order services for both branches and single-plant firms tend to be provided in the local area, except around Toronto which has a shadow effect on the surrounding region with both branches and single-plant firms looking to the metropolitan area. At greater distances, the local town is more important for higher-order services for single-unit firms than for branches, even though it may be poorly endowed with such services. In fact a recent Norwegian study has indicated that in less accessible areas management tends to use low-order service functions to provide high-level services—e.g. the local bank manager is asked to give advice on long-range financial planning. Even though services may be available locally, branches tend to be steered towards Oslo while single-unit firms are often unaware of the existence of potential service linkages in nearby towns. Functional connections across the hierarchy at the lower levels are therefore weakly developed.

As a result of such behaviour major cities which are the loci of the head offices of corporate organizations have naturally become the control or steering centres for the urban system. The increasing concentration of economic activity into a limited number of such organizations has tended to reinforce this process of spatial concentration of control and the resulting disparities in regional development (cf. Parsons, 1972; Watts, 1972; Westaway, 1974b). The regional implications of the development of organizations from small single-function firms through national organizations engaged in several activities in many regions to multi-divisional and finally multi-national corporations have been discussed by Westaway. The growth of national corporations has involved on the one hand a horizontal division of management into specialist department finance, personnel, purchasing, sales, etc.—and a vertical system of contro designed to connect and co-ordinate departments. In particular the head office's responsibility has been to co-ordinate, appraise, and plan for the survival and growth of a corporation as a whole. Growth through mergers and takeovers tend to lead to a concentration of office employment as dup cated functions which existed in the separate organizations prior to amalga mation are eliminated. External services that smaller organizations had to contract out are internalized because they can now be provided economically for the larger group. In the multi-divisional corporation, each division is concerned with one product line and is supervised by its own divisional head office, while a group head office plans for the enterprise as a whole.

In order to see how the development of the corporate hierarchy relates to the spatial concentration of control, Westaway draws attention to three levels of business administration, three time horizons, three levels of task, and three levels of decision-making within an organization which have a bearing on location.

In the early stages of corporate development, i.e. the small single-function single-unit firm of classic location theory, all three levels are embodied in one entrepreneur. As the company expands into a national corporation, level three, which is concerned with the day-to-day management of production, is separated both functionally and geographically from the higher levels. Level two would be concerned with the medium-term co-ordination of a number of production plants probably from a head office located in an accessible large city. Level one compromises top management whose function is to determine long-term goals and plan company strategy, thereby setting a framework within which all other levels operate. In the multi-divisional corporation this highest level may be separated from level two in the form of a group head office located in a capital city—principally because of the need for close connections with the money market, the media, and government.

Information flows and office location

It is parly because of different needs for contacts, both within the organization and with the outside world, that units at different levels in a company may be located in different types of geographical environment. The Swedish geographer, Gunnar Törnqvist, has explicitly linked one hierarchical model of organizational structure to the volume of information flows within and between organizations (Fig. 2.2). The organization is divided into control functions (the circle) and production functions (the square); the control or administrative functions are in turn divided into three levels. Because of their different contact requirements and the relative importance of different methods of communication, these various functions have different location patterns. Törnqvist has

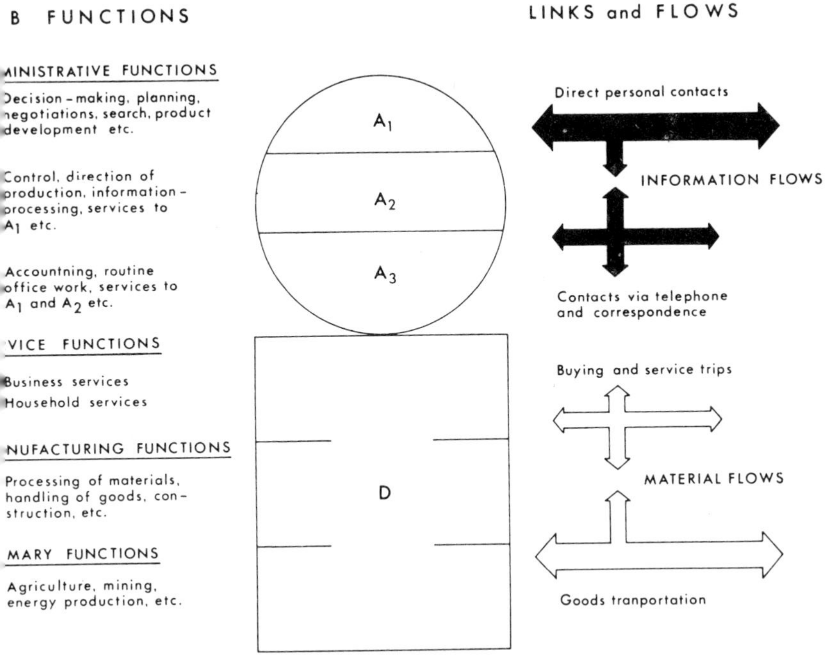

Fig. 2.2. Diagrammatic representation of an activity system consisting of job functions connected by links and flows.
(from Törnqvist, 1973)

demonstrated this by describing the changing distribution of employment in various occupational levels in Sweden and relating these changes to data on average frequency of face-to-face contacts obtained from a national survey of airline passengers (Törnqvist, 1970; Sahlberg, 1970; Engström, 1970). Table 2.1 shows that it is the highest-level jobs that involve the most personal contacts with other organizations, and, as we have seen in Chapter 1, it is the highest-level administrative functions which have been growing most rapidly in the three largest cities of Stockholm, Gothenburg, and Malmo.

The attractiveness of the large cities for such functions can be seen principally in terms of contact possibilities with the rest of the country *i* and with all the other organizations that are also located in the city *ii* itself, i.e. interregional and intra-urban contact. Interregional contact possibilities are particularly a function of the organization of the national passenger transport systems, which tend to focus heavily on the capital. Törnqvist has modified the concept of population potential to derive an index of contact possibilities which takes account of the distribution of contact-intensive occupations and travel time between city regions (Fig. 2.3). The index is based upon the number of hours of personal contact in a single day that can be had with people working in another region, averaged over all regions. The index number illustrate the dominance

TABLE 2.1

Number of contacts and time spent in contacts by employees in eight administrative job levels in seven organizations in Sweden

	Job level							
	1	2	3	4	5	6	7	8
No. of contacts per empl. per week	19	10	6	3	2	–	–	–
No. of hours spent in contact per empl. per week	37	20	12	5	3	–	–	–

Source: Törnqvist (1970).

of Stockholm. Its position is further reinforced if account is taken of the possibility for connections to international contacts. It is both a cause and a consequence of such contact possibilities that organizations place their highest-level functions in the capital city (Törnqvist, 1973; Engström and Sahlberg, 1973).

This emphasis on the regional system should not obscure the fact that in absolute terms the great majority of contacts are with the town within which a particular office is located. This appears to be the case regardless of the size of the city itself. A number of studies of actual (as opposed to potential) contact patterns have demonstrated this. Studies of organizations with head offices located in different towns in Sweden have shown that between 40 and 50 per cent of all time spent on personal external contacts are with persons working in the immediate vicinity (Törnqvist, 1970; Hedberg, 1970) (Fig. 2.4). These figures are substantially different only for organizations located in Stockholm where the city itself is able to satisfy nearly three-quarters of all external contact needs. After the local town, Stockholm is the leading source for external contacts of firms located elsewhere. There are very few links across the urban hierarchy at lower levels. The picture that emerges is one of an urban system composed of discrete and remarkably self-contained centres.

The importance of the near environment is also demonstrated by a number of other studies. A communication survey of a 100 office establishments located in four different urban regions of Sweden has shown that 76 per cent of all contacts with other organizations involved travel to places less than 30 minutes' journey away (Thorngren, 1973). Another survey of 115 offices throughout the U.K. conducted for the Post Office has indicated that 70 per cent of meetings involving persons from other establishments give rise to journeys of less than 30 minutes (Connell, 1973). These similarities seem to occur irrespective of differences in the density of contact opportunities. In the heart of central London a survey of commercial offices has shown that 78 per cent of all business journeys last less than 30 minutes (Goddard, 1973a). But there

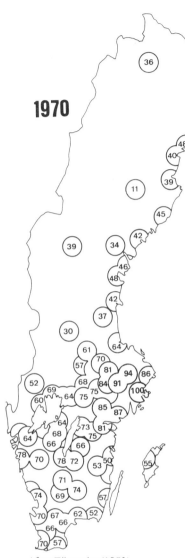

1970

Fig. 2.3. Contact potentials for major urban region in Sweden
Notes: Figures are index numbers with Stockholm = 100, and are based upon a measure of accessibility from each urban region to potential contact sources in the remaining 70 regions. Potential (P_i) are calculated according to the formula:

$$P_i = \sum_{j=1}^{70} (T_{ij} - D_{ij}) K_j$$

where: T_{ij} = length of time in a single working day it is possible to remain in region j after a journey from region i;

D_{ij} = travel time by shortest route from region i to region j;

K_j = total number of persons employed in j in contact intensive job functions in region j, weighted by the national average daily hours of contact for each job function.

After Törnqvist (1973).

is one important difference between central London and the other examples quoted, that is <u>the diversity of potential contacts with highly qualified people that can be made for a given length of journey in the city centre compared with elsewhere</u>. The <u>*quality* of the information</u> obtained in the capital city is therefore as potentially important as its <u>*quantity.*</u>

The Swedish economist, Bertil Thorngren, has discussed in some detail the significance of different types of information for the development

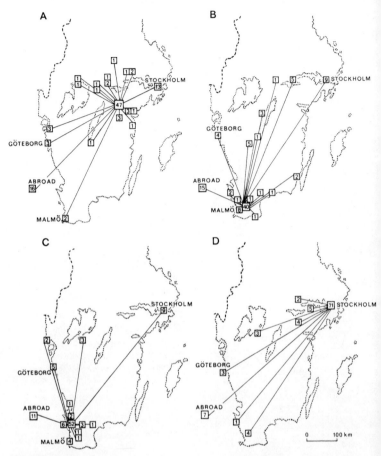

Fig. 2.4. Percentage breakdown of contact time by destination centres, in Sweden. (from Törnqvist 1970)

of organizations and regions (Fig. 2.5). He has related this to the process by which organizations achieve external economies by locating offices and productive units in different regions (Thorngren, 1967, 1968). It is well known that considerable direct financial savings can be gained by <u>contracting out business services</u> like accountancy rather than providing these within the organization. The link between the administrative part of the organization (the circle in Fig. 2.5) and the other firms that provide these services consists of information flows paralleled by monetary flows. Such pecuniary economies are equivalent to those gained by contracting out part of the production process from the manufacturing unit (the square in Fig. 2.5). In this case material flows are paralleled by monetary flows and of course information flows of a rather routine nature. But perhaps the most <u>important</u> external economies are those associated with perhaps chance information about new markets, supplie

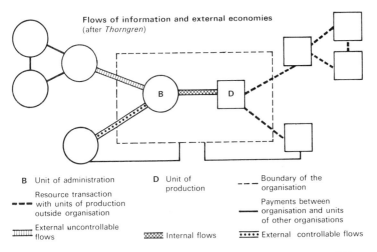

Fig. 2.5. Flows of information and external economies (from Thorngren 1970).

<u>production process</u>, etc., information which in the long run could be essential to the survival of the organization.

The fact that some contacts are unrelated to the day-to-day processes of buying and selling introduces the notion that different contacts might be related to different time horizons. While some may be concerned with current matters other are likely to involve long-term issues.

Information flows and regional and organizational development processes

A number of writers have stressed the importance of information flows as a key process in the long-term development of organizations. For example, Steed (1971, pp. 207—8) notes 'To obtain some understanding of the manner whereby [organizations] adapt to changing conditions, we must indicate the range of their information inputs and their processes of decision making.' Here the 'process of decision making' refers to the way in which information from the outside environment is channelled through the organization, hopefully to the places where appropriate action can be taken. Following Aguilar (1967) and Dill (1962), Steed suggests that an understanding of this process involves discovering how organizations scan their environment and their modes of scanning, particularly 'which mode is associated with what information needs, how mode assignments are made and what procedures operate to alter their rules of scanning'.

Thorngren (1970) has suggested three principal modes by which organizations scan their environment. He divides the environment into two halves—a knowledge and a values environment (Fig. 2.6). Each part of the environment is in turn divided into a series of distinct time horizons. The first type of interaction between the organization and its environment,

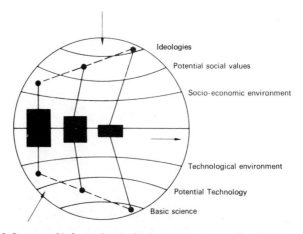

Fig. 2.6. Sources of information in the development space (from Thorngren, 1970)

i referred to as 'orientation' processes by Thorngren, links the furthest segments of the knowledge and values environment (basic sciences and ideology). This type of relation concerns the very long-run future of the organization. In the case of a motor-car manufacturer this might involve considerations of developments in basic science that could provide an alternative to the car and possible changes in societal values with respect

ii to personal mobility. The second type of relation or 'planning' processes link potential social values and technology and involve the development of specific products identified by earlier orientation relations. Planning relations involve a less random scanning of the environment than orientation processes. In the case of the car manufacturer these processes may involve the development of, say, a battery-operated vehicle. Finally, the bulk of an organization's external relations operate within established technological and social environments and are concerned with the control

iii of existing resources. These 'programmed' relations are structured according to a pattern laid down by earlier orientation and planning relations. In the case of the car manufacturer such relations might be concerned with producing next year's models.

The important point for regional and organizational development is that these three processes tend to involve different contact networks or 'modes of scanning', with some types of spatial environment being more appropriate for one type of contact than another. Thorngren suggests that orientation relations tend to take place in large pre-arranged meetings involving wide-ranging discussions between people often coming into contact for the first time. It is the widening or divergent character of the contact network that distinguishes orientation processes. Only the largest metropolises offer the wide range of potential contacts with government, researchers, financial institutions, and other business organizations, contacts which are essential for the conduct of orientation processes (Meir 1962).

Planning processes, on the other hand, tend to involve limited sets of familiar individuals, each with more clearly defined objectives and information search tasks. Unlike orientation, planning activities are less dependent on random contact: indeed the great variety of information thrown up in the large metropolis may conflict with the development of a specific project and lead to communications overload. Being familiar with one another, individuals involved in planning contacts can use telecommunications, provided there are opportunities for regular (e.g. monthly) personal meetings. The location of research and development activities in relatively remote locations in the Outer South East of England is remarkably consistent with this theory.

Finally, the great majority of external relations are concerned with routine matters. They involve specific discussions between familiar participants who are in frequent contact usually about matters directly related to buying or selling. Theoretically there is no reason why such activities could not be conducted in relatively remote locations using telecommunications. However, the sheer volume of contact may prevent this. Because of their routine nature these types of contacts in particular are likely to be strongly affected by distance and, therefore, to be confined to the local environment.

Obviously all individuals and organizations located in different urban regions are involved in these three types of processes and communication to varying degress. However, the greater opportunities for orientation contacts provided by the largest urban regions do give organizations located in these areas considerable advantages in terms of short-run non-pecuniary external economies, which in the long run may lead to more readily measurable benefits such as higher levels of productivity. Although orientation contacts may be required at relatively infrequent intervals, the difficulty of making contact with the centre from a remote urban area may deter these connections altogether. The fact that an individual might have to travel half a day in order to attend a meeting may mean that this link is not made and a vital opportunity for learning about some new process is lost. What is even more likely is that the businessman in peripheral areas is not aware of the sources of information that are available elsewhere. Ultimately such considerations could account for the observed poorer performance of firms in peripheral regions.

Conclusion: office employment, the key to regional and urban development problems

This chapter has taken a very broad view of office employment. Rather than examining office development as a purely physical phenomenon or type of employment, we have emphasized the role performed by different office functions within large organizations with units located in a number of cities. Such organizations, be they in the public or private sector, in manufacturing industry, commerce, or both, are coming to dominate modern society. In many respects location theory is still in the age of the first industrial revolution and has not adjusted itself to the realities of the post industrial age in which office activities and large organizations rather than single unit manufacturing firms dominate the scene. As organizations continue to grow in size and economic and social life becomes increasingly complex, we can be certain that more and more people will be involved in the management of this size and complexity—that is in office-type jobs.

When we come to examine the economic and social consequences of such tendencies a number of undesirable side-effects become apparent, especially if we adopt a viewpoint which stresses the need for equality of opportunity for individuals living in different parts of the country. The concentration of economic power into a few large organizations has also been paralleled by a geographical concentration of higher-level employment opportunities into a few regions, a process which has important implications for occupational mobility on the one hand and the economic development of small organizations outside the corporate hierarchy on the other.

3 Office location in the city centre

Introduction

Chapter 1 has demonstrated the growing importance of office employment nationally and Chapter 2 has suggested how the geographical concentration of higher-level office functions could be fundamental to problems of regional development. Although in policy terms it is now widely appreciated that office jobs can make significant contributions towards solving regional employment problems, very little is known about the nature of the ties that confined one out of every seven office workers in England and Wales in 1966 to the ten square miles of Central London.

Such figures immediately raise the question of how essential it is for all of this office employment to be so concentrated, and make the assessment of locational priorities a matter of national important. In Britain, central government controls on office development have been in operation in London and the South-East since 1964, yet few objective criteria have been formulated to assess the appropriateness of one type of office activity or another for a central location. Similarly, within Greater London, the Greater London Development Plan has declared as a key objective that 'the activities that need to be in Central London should be given opportunity to develop' (G.L.C. 1970), but while it recognizes the need for a selective approach towards planning the economic structure of Central London, there is at present little evidence as to what activities should be encouraged or discouraged and by what criteria appropriateness for the centre is to be assessed.

So while Chapter 2 has emphasized the importance of linkages between cities and spatially separate parts of large organizations as a framework for understanding regional and corporate development processes, this chapter emphasises the measurement of links between office establishments within cities—what Jean Gottman has called the 'interweaving of quarternary functions'—as a basis for identifying the nature of ties of offices to the city centre (Gottman 1970).

The importance of such intra-urban linkages should have been apparent in the previous discussion of regional development issues. Empirically, the pronounced effect of distance on flows of information suggests the importance of intra-urban contacts. Theoretically, Warneryd's model of interdependence in urban systems draws attention to linkages between the administrative offices of large firms and independent service agencies in the same city. Thorngren's model of regional external economies furthermore suggests that in addition to ease of contact with specialist services, a central location increases the chance of non-commercial linkages which can be vital for the long-run development of an organiz ation. The likelihood of information being obtained in this way is muc greater in an urban agglomeration where complexes of interlinked activities can be found.

Such complexes of office activities (the cluster of circles in Fig. 2.5 are analogous to industrial complexes where productive activities are linked by material flows (the cluster of squares in Fig. 2.5). In the offi complex information 'produced' by one office establishment may the fore be the input to another. However, for a 'complex' to exist, certair establishments must be closely linked to one another but weakly con- nected with establishments that fall into other groups.

A number of approaches both direct and indirect can be made to the identification of such complexes and the measurement of the strength of the linkages binding office establishments together within the city centre. The direct approach involves obtaining data on the amount and type of contact between different office functions. Owing to the pronounced effect of distance on personal contacts (within Central London a third of all business journeys are on foot and 38 per cent take less than 10 minutes) there will be a propensity for closely linked office establishments to locate near to one another in the city centre. So analysis of patterns of spatial association can be used to in- directly suggest functional connection. Finally, the pattern of physical movement between locations within the city centre will reflect the functional linkages between geographically separated activities.

The structure of city centre linkages

This threefold approach to the analysis of activity linkages and urba structure is suggested by the pioneering work of Rannells and Webber (Rannels 1956; Webber 1964). The manner in which this sort of frame work may operate is suggested by the work of Berry, not in the contex of urban analysis but in terms of the relationship between commodity flows between sectors and regions and the spatial structure of the natic economy (Berry 1966). Following Berry's approach, data on city cent linkages may be arranged in three matrices: (1) an inter-sector input-ou matrix of information flows; (2) a spatial structure matrix describing t geographical distribution of office employment in different sectors between different locations (areal units); (3) a matrix of the physical movements between these locations (Fig. 3.1).

Of course these matrices may be further disaggregated. Information flows can be classified according to their type and their associated com munication channel (e.g. paper flows, personal contacts involving trave and electronic communications like telephone and telex.) The matrices may also be related to one another both emprically and theoretically ir order to improve our understanding of the connection between locatio

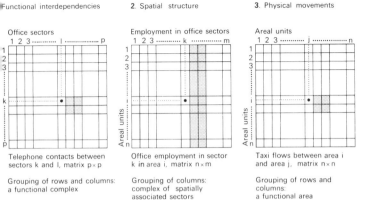

Fig. 3.1. Components of the city centre office linkage system.

patterns, movements, and functional linkages. Specifically, one may ask to what extent patterns of spatial association call forth correspondingly structured patterns of internal circulation and how far both reflect the functional groupings of office sectors. The data and the insights they provide may finally be used in a policy context to suggest those sectors which are weakly linked both spatially and functionally to the city centre system and are therefore likely candidates for decentralization.

Office complexes: a functional approach

The first and perhaps fundamental matrix that we shall examine is that describing the pattern of information flows between different office sectors (Goddard 1973a). In 1970 contact data were obtained from a sample of 72 office establishments from a cross-section of the business sectors of Central London. Within these establishments, samples of businessmen in different departments recorded details of their telephone calls and meetings with persons from other firms over a period of three days in a specially designed contact diary. Amongst other things respondents were asked to record against each contact the nature of business of the firms of the people with whom they had spoken. Firms were allocated to 42 business sectors. From the data, two matrices describing the number of telephone and meeting contacts between pairs of sectors could be constructed.

The object of the analysis of these matrices was to identify sectors with similar patterns of functional linkages. By correlating the columns of the matrix it is possible to identify pairs of sectors which receive information from similar types of establishment. Factor analysis of this correlation matrix will indicate groups of sectors with similar linkage patterns: high factor loadings reveal the sectors receiving information from common sources; high factor scores identify these sources.

Owing to the specific nature of inter-office complementarities, certain office sectors are closely linked to one another but have weaker connections

TABLE 3.1

Three Central London office complexes identified through factor analysis of inter-sectoral telephone calls

Civil engineering

Destination sector	F.L.	Origin sector	F.S.
Architects	0·87	General construction Cos.	5·1
General construction Cos.	0·84	Consulting engineers	1·4
Consulting engineers	0·83	Bricks, pottery glass, cement	1·3
Specialist construction Cos.	0·76		
Metal and metal goods	0·69		
Primary industry	0·67		
Bricks, pottery, glass, cement	0·66		

Explained variance 12·54%

Banking and finance

Destination sector	F.L.	Origin sector	F.S.
Stockbroking	−0·89	Banking	−3·8
Property	−0·87	Property	−4·3
Banking	−0·86		
Legal services	−0·85		
Other finance	−0·66		
Accounting	−0·52		

Explained variance 10·56%

Commodity building

Destination sector	F.L.	Origin sector	F.S.
Food wholesaling	−0·79	Export and import merchants	−4·9
Textile, leather, clothing	−0·77	Property Cos.	−4·4
Export and import merchants	−0·61	Commodity brokers	−1·4
Transport services	−0·60	Food wholesaling	−1·8
		Retailing	−1·0

Explained variance 6·70%

Notes
1. Only three of the six identifiable functional clusters are listed: these six together account for 62·05% of the variance in the inter-sectoral telephone ca.
2. F.L. = Factor loading.   F.S. = Factor score.
3. Only factor loadings (which indicate the importance of each sector as a destination for contacts in the cluster) greater than ± 0·50 and factor scores (which indicate the degree of importance of each sector as an origin for conta in the cluster) greater than ± 1·00 are listed.

Source: Goddard 1973a.

with sectors that fall into other groups. Information flows between office sectors are therefore far from random. As a result factor analysis of the inter-sectoral telephone-call matrix identifies six groups which account for 62 per cent of total variations in the pattern of calls. Table 3.1 describes three such groups: civil engineering, banking and finance, and commodity trading. The former includes architects, consulting engineers, and brick and cement manufacturers. The group focuses on general construction companies from which most contacts originate. It is well known that many aspects of a civil engineering project are contracted out to different types of firms; inevitably this procedure will lead to a substantial amount of personal contact between the various contractors.

Factor analysis is inclined to give the impression that the various complexes are closed systems with little or no inter-connection between office sectors falling into the different groups. Fig. 3.2 reveals that this is far from the case. In this diagram sectors are assigned to groups suggested by the factor analysis. A heavy line indicates that both of the sectors that it links directed 50 per cent more contacts to each other than would be expected given their respective shares of all recorded contacts. A lighter line represents a one-way relationship in the direction of the arrow.[†] Examination of Fig. 3.2 reveals that all sectors within the cluster are not necessarily linked to each other by reciprocated information flows; in addition to within-group linkages there are also significant links between groups. For example, the category of transport services (18) has links with export and import merchants (23) and commodity brokers (24) in the civil engineering group. These links between as well as within clearly definable spheres of business activities suggest that individual office sectors frequently perform diverse functions.

Fig. 3.2 also indicates the importance of indirect linkage knitting together otherwise independent subgroupings. For example, it is well known that a firm wishing to place an advertisement usually approaches the media such as a newspaper publisher through an advertising agency. In Fig. 3.2 links via architects (34) and property companies (30) connect together financial and engineering groups which are centred on banking (27) and construction companies (14).

In view of this very complex pattern of linkages, policies of controlling office development and of office dispersal need to be managed with considerable care. If employment in an activity that was central to a

† This type of analysis measuring the *relative impact* of one sector upon another is referred to as transaction flow analysis (Savage and Deutsch 1960). For example if Sector i generated 10% of all contacts in Central London it would be *expected* to direct 10% of this total Sector j; if it directed 20% or more of its *actual* contact to Sector j this would be represented by a light line in Fig. 3.2. If j in turn directed a disproportionate share of its contact to i the relationship is reciprocated and shown by a heavy line. Clearly the 50% threshold is an arbitrary measure of the significant differences between observed and expected flows.

complex were to decline through planning intervention the external economies the complex offers to its members could be undermined. On the other hand increases in employment in sectors that are weakly connected could have undesired side-effects on other activities by adding unnecessarily to the congestion costs of the city centre in terms of higher prices for land, labour, and other economic factors.

The information obtained in the analysis of inter-sectoral contact flows can therefore be used to provide a number of indicators on which a policy of selective decentralization could be based. These could include measures of the <u>extent to which a sector is involved in one or more functional complexes;</u> measures of indirect linkages to other sectors; and measures of the extent to which contacts are confined to a limited number of other sectors. Such data can also be used to suggest how complexes of related office activities can be established in alternative office centres outside the capital through the relocation of groups of interlinked

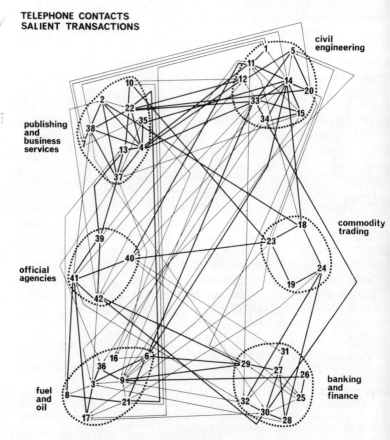

TELEPHONE CONTACTS
SALIENT TRANSACTIONS

unctions and the local encouragement of specific activities needed to
complete a particular complex.

Office complexes: a spatial approach

These results raise the question of how far groups of functionally
related office sectors are also associated with one another spatially, being
ied not only to other firms in the city centre at large but also to particu-
ar locations within it. Flows of information that depend on personal
contact may encourage the linked activities to locate close to one
another even inside the city centre.

The spatial association of office activities may be measured by correlating the distribution of employment in different sectors over a series
of areal units. Here we use 64 employment categories and 69 traffic
ones. These zones are designed to be as internally homogeneous as
possible in their employment structure. Approximately 2000 pairs of
relationships can be examined in this way, and 73 sectors are positively
associated with a correlation value of 0·50 or above. Many pairs of
ectors are therefore unrelated to each other in their geographical dis-
ribution *at this scale* of sectoral and geographical disaggregation.

We can unravel some of the complexities in patterns of spatial
association through the use of factor analysis which identifies groups of
ectors with similar geographical distributions. Table 3.2 describes three
uch groups. The trading cluster, for example, is composed of establishments highly localized in the City of London, including transport services,

---

Fig. 3.2. Inter-sectoral telephone contacts in Central London (from Goddard 1973a)
Key:

1. Primary industry
2. Food, drink and tobacco
3. Fuel and oil
4. Chemicals
5. Metals and metal goods
6. Mechanical engineering and machinery
7. Precision engineering
8. Electrical engineering
9. Transport equipment
10. Textiles, leather and clothing
11. Bricks, pottery, glass and cement
12. Other manufacturing
13. Paper, printing and publishing
14. General construction
15. Specialist contracting
16. Gas, electricity and water
17. Transport and communications
18. Transport services
19. Food wholesaling
20. Other specialist wholesaling
21. General wholesale merchants
22. Retailing
23. Export and import merchants
24. Commodity brokers
25. Insurance companies
26. Other insurance
27. Banking
28. Stockbroking and jobbing
29. Other finance
30. Property
31. Accounting
32. Legal services
33. Consulting engineers
34. Architects
35. Other specialist consultancy
36. Non-profit services
37. Advertising and public relations
38. Miscellaneous business services
39. Broadcasting
40. Public authorities
41. Central government
42. Local government

TABLE 3.2

Three Central London office complexes identified through factor analysis of spatial distribution of employment in different office sectors

Trading	F.L
Agriculture, forestry, and fishing	−0·8⟨
Food	−0·68
Transport	−0·6(
Postal services and telecommunications	−0·9⟨
Transport services	−0·9⟨
Food wholesaling	−0·7⟨
General wholesale merchants	−0·8⟨
Export and import merchants	−0·6(
Commodity brokers, merchants, and dealers	−0·9⟨
Other insurance	−0·9⟨

(Explained variance = 18·54%)

Civil engineering	F.L
Bricks, pottery, glass, cement	−0·7⟨
General construction and contracting	−0·6(
Specialist contracting	−0·5⟨
Consulting engineers	−0·7⟨
Architects	−0·5⟨
Other specialist consultants	−0·6⟨
Employers' and trade associations	−0·8⟨
Professional membership organizations	−0·5⟨
Charitable organizations	−0·7⟨

(Explained variance = 7·45%)

Banking and Finance	F.L
Insurance companies	0·8⟨
Central banking	0·8⟨
Other banking	0·8⟨
Stockbroking and jobbing	0·8⟨
Other finance	0·7⟨
Accounting, auditing, and book-keeping	0·9⟨
Legal services	0·5⟨
Office services	0·6⟨
Head offices of offices operating abroad	0·6⟨

(Explained variance = 6·84%)

Notes:

1. Only three of the five identifiable spatial clusters are linked: these five together account for 50·78% of spatial variation in the distribution of office employme⟨
2. F.L. = Factor Loading.
3. Only factor loadings greater than ± 0·50 are shown. These indicate the degree of association of each sector with the respective cluster.

Source: Goddard 1973a

risk insurance, commodity trading, and export-import merchants. This cluster is the spatial equivalent of the commodity trading group identified in the analysis of telephone calls. The functional distinction betwe⟨

the trading and financial activities of the City is reinterpreted in spatial terms. Here we see that insurance companies as a whole are more strongly associated with banking and finance while other insurance such as insurance broking is associated with the trading group.

We can identify the areas in which office employment in the sectors associated with each cluster is localized by drawing maps of factor scores. Two such maps are reproduced in Fig. 3.3. Here we see that employment in activities related to the civil engineering complex can be found principally in Westminster and Bloomsbury and banking and finance in the City of London.

Office complexes: a movement approach

Functional linkages between geographically separated office establishments will give rise to physical movements which should be structured in a way that reflects the location of linked activities. After walking, the taxi is the most important mode of business travel in central London, accounting for about a quarter of all such trips. We can again use factor analysis to explore the pattern of inter-zonal taxi flows in central London, with the provisio that these flows do include trips for non-business purposes. High factor loadings indicate groups of traffic zones with taxis arriving from common origins: high factor scores specify these origins. By linking the two together on a map we can identify movement sub-systems or functional regions within central London. (Fig. 3.4).

Altogether five such sub-systems can be identified which correspond closely to the various districts that contain groups of functionally linked businesses. The five sub-systems are the West End (clothing and business services); Westminster (civil engineering and central government); Fleet Street, Covent Garden, and Soho (publishing and entertainment); the City (trading, banking, and finance), and Bloomsbury (civil engineering and the University). As in the analysis of functional and spatial complexes there is some degree of overlap between some of the sub-systems (for example, the West End and Westminster), while others are more separate (e.g. Westminster and the City).

Office complexes in the city centre: a conclusion

While similarities have been stressed there is not a complete one-to-one relationship between office location, functional linkages and movement patterns in the city centre. In part this is due to the inconsistencies in the original data.[†] Nevertheless, the differences between the various

† Some sectors are over-represented and others under-represented in the sample survey of business contacts; further, a much coarser sectoral disaggregation had to be applied to these data than those referring to location patterns. Finally, the data on taxi movements do not separately distinguish trips generated by commercial offices and those associated with other activities, such as the University, government offices, hotels, places of entertainment, and shops.

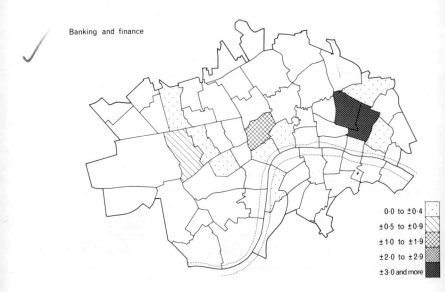

Banking and finance

0·0 to ±0·4
±0·5 to ±0·9
±1·0 to ±1·9
±2·0 to ±2·9
±3·0 and more

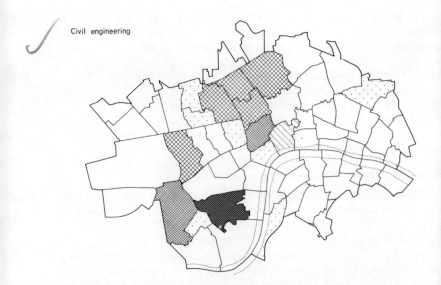

Civil engineering

Fig. 3.3. The distribution of Central London office employment in the civil engineering and banking finance complexes as indicated by factor scores (from Goddard 1973a).

· Factor loading >0·5
O Factor score   >1·0

· Factor loading >0·5
O Factor score   >1·0

Fig. 3.4. Two movement complexes in Central London (The City above, Bloomsbury below) identified by factor analysis of inter-zonal taxi flows (compare to Fig. 3.3.) (from Goddard 1970b).

systems also reflect the very real fact that spatial association is not a necessary condition for functional linkage. This is perhaps increasingly the case as the physical constraints on contacts are reduced through developments in communications technology. As will be described in the next section, many activities associated with traditional spatial complexes are moving from these areas both to other locations with Central London and outside the centre altogether. This is partly because the functional linkages that bind the activities into the complex are maintained by a network of very routine contacts and can therefore be satisfactorily performed by telecommunications over some distance. The strength as opposed to the pattern of these office linkages will be discussed further in Chapter 5.

In spite of all this, the continuing interconnection between functional linkages, location, and movement within the city centre cannot be denied. Some activities are clearly tied not only to the city centre at large but to particular sub-areas within it. These sub-areas or office districts appear to be maintained by a strong pattern of internal circulation. Such findings have particular significance for planning the spatial structure of the city centre: if functionally linked activities can be encouraged to locate in particular sub-areas, movement will be minimized and external economies increased.

Changing office location patterns

The proceeding discussion has been based entirely on a cross-sectional analysis of office location patterns and linkages at one point in time. It would be wrong to assume that such relationships will remain fixed in the future. As the economy evolves, new types and combinations of office activities will develop with new locational requirements to match. At the same time developments in communications technology will modify the need for close spatial proximity.

This certainly appears to be the case according to the historical record of changing office location patterns in Central London (Goddard 1967). If we examine the location of publishers' offices over a 50-year period since the end of the First World War very marked changes can be observed.

In 1918 publishers could be found in two distinct concentrations: one around St. Paul's (E.C.4) and the other in the vicinity of Covent Garden (W.C.2). By 1938 a second cluster around the British Museum (W.C.1) was well developed but there were already signs of this pattern and concentration breaking down with several firms locating further west outside 'the trade area'. By 1966 publishers occupied locations throughout a much larger central business district: although the trade clusters remain they are no longer so dominant. In addition, 19 per cent of publishers in the London postal area were located outside the centre

in 1966 compared with only 2 per cent in 1918. The fact that considerable external economies can be made in publishing by the use of specialist services such as wholesale book counters, accounts for the importance
of nucleated trade areas at the beginning of the period. The changes
observed since then would suggest that these benefits are no longer so
important or do not require such a high degree of concentration.

Only a small part of these aggregate location changes can be attributed
to the movement of firms between different locations: the establishment
of new offices in particular areas and the closure of existing offices elsewhere is a far more important component of change. Of a net increase
of 53 publishers' offices in West One between 1951 and 1966 only 12
had been located in another postal district at the beginning of the period.
Likewise the establishment of new firms outside the centre has accounted
for nearly half the total increase of publishers in the rest of London,
although 24 of the firms existing both in 1951 and 1966 had in fact
decentralized.

The high turnover rate of office establishments is not unexpected
given that the majority are extremely small. In 1970, 55 per cent of all
establishments in the paper, printing, and publishing sector employed
fewer than 10 people. In fact only 32 of all the publishers in existence
in Central London in 1918 had survived until 1966. Book publishing
in particular consists of a core of long-established firms about which a
large number come and go, only a small proportion surviving to be
successful entrants to the trade. This high mortality rate is characteristic
of a number of sectors: it would seem that the office population of the
city centre at any one time consists of a large number of very small
businesses which never get off the ground. Those that survive expand
and have to make a large number of moves in search of more appropriate
accommodation. For example, between 1918 and 1966 one advertising
agency made 10 moves, most of them over very short distances. Another
made a number of moves within the centre before leaving Central London
altogether. Decentralization should therefore be seen as part of the
natural evolution of an office organization with certain activities being
hived off to more appropriate environments. In the next chapter we go
on to consider policies that have aimed at influencing this pattern of
decentralization. But before proceeding it should be remembered from
this analysis that relocation is only a small component of aggregate shifts
in the geographical distribution of office activities.

4 Office location policy in Britain

Introduction

As in many areas of public life, office location policy in Britain has been subject to two sometimes contradictory pulls. On the one hand there has been a need to deal with the problems of imbalance in the dis tribution of opportunity between major regions of the country—namely the South East and the Midlands *vis-à-vis* the development areas—and o the other the need to combat congestion in London. The distribution o office activities is fundamental to both of these problems, but partly as result of the very obvious concentration of office development in the centre of London, policy has until recently concentrated on shifting office employment away from this area, with very little concern as to where it was relocated. The movement of offices from the South East a a whole to regions not so well endowed with office employment was in the first instance seen to be of secondary importance. This was partly because long-distance movement of offices was deemed to be impractic

However, as the significance of office employment to regional devel ment began to be appreciated, restrictive measures designed to encoura longer-distance movement of offices (that is between rather than withi regions), were introduced. In the absence of strong financial inducemer for firms to move to the development areas, these restrictions have had the probable effect of discouraging short-distance movement both with the Greater London conurbation and to other areas in the South East while doing little to encourage office development outside the South East (Rhodes and Kan 1971). Criticism of the negative outcome of the conflicting policy objectives has recently led to the introduction of ne measures aimed at removing some of the obstacles to long-distance mo ment to the development areas. Nevertheless the underlying conflict between and intra- and interregional objectives still remains.

Office location policy prior to 1964

Until 1964 the issue of office development was essentially a local matter controlled through the normal physical planning machinery. In so far as this process was overseen by central government, office develo ment was the responsibility of the Ministry of Housing and Local Gove ment (now the Department of the Environment). In contrast, industria development has been strictly controlled by central government (the Board of Trade) through Industrial Development Certificates. This was consistent with the evolution of regional policy based on the analysis o the 1939 Barlow Report (significantly entitled the Royal Commission on the Distribution of the *Industrial* Population) which associated problems of regional imbalance *and* urban congestion with the location of manufacturing activities. So alongside control on industrial development in the so-called congested regions, the Board of Trade also offered substantial financial inducements for manufacturing plants to be moved to development areas. These two sets of policy instruments (controls and inducements) were designed to meet the twin objectives of industrial decentralization from the major conurbations, especially London and Birmingham, and interregional redistribution of manufacturing activities.

What the Barlow Report and the plans for reshaping London that emerged from it both failed to appreciate was that the main component of growth in London and the South East region would be office rather than manufacturing activities. This became readily apparent in the middle fifties when the full impact of the post-war rebuilding of central London, coupled with the relaxation of physical planning controls, began to be felt. As a result of war damage, office floor space in central London had been reduced from around 87 million square feet to 78 million square feet. By 1955 approval had been given for no less than 28 million square feet, nearly 3 times as much as was lost by war damage (Cowan *et al.* 1969).

In response to the obvious congestion that was resulting from a massive influx of office workers into the Central Area, the local planning authorities (London, Middlesex, and subsequently Kent, Surrey, and Essex County Councils) began to encourage office decentralization to surburban London by restricting the number of planning permissions granted for office developments inside the centre while being more liberal with permissions outside it. In so doing they were probably according with a natural tendency for office development to spread outside the centre (cf. Marriott 1967). The combined effect of this natural tendency and the encouragement of planning policy was that office development was scattered across the face of suburban London: very little new office development occurred in Inner London outside the centre. The only suburban concentration of office space was in Croydon where the local corporation deliberately set out to encourage the development of a major office centre, coupling this with major transportation improvements and a shopping precinct.

By the late 1950s a substantial amount of office space was being given planning permission outside the centre of London. However, there was still strong pressure for office development in the Central Area which the L.C.C. found hard to resist. By 1963 a further 32 million square feet of office space had been approved. The central government attempted to head off some of this demand in 1964 with the foundation of a quasi-independent Location of Offices Bureau (L.O.B.). The role of the Bureau was (and still is) entirely advisory and confined to promoting the movement of offices from Central London. The Bureau had no authority to encourage movement to any particular area outside of Central London, although as an agent of central government with its concern for development areas as well as the problems of congestion in Central London, it was bound to pay some attention to promoting the case of these areas.

Office location and regional policy, 1964–1973

After the tentative move in this direction represented by the L.O.B., a new government fully entered the office location arena in 1964 with the imposition of a ban on office development in the whole of the London region and the West Midlands conurbation. Developers wishing to build offices, initially involving more than 3000 square feet of space, first had to obtain an office development permit from the government as well as normal planning permission from the local authority. In applying for a permit, the developer had to argue that the occupier of the proposed office space was tied to London and could not operate elsewhere. As the developer had to have a particular client in view, this made speculative development in advance of acquiring tenants difficult. The criteria laid down by the government therefore explicity acknowledged the importance of linkages in assessing the need for a London location, but in the absence of any hard evidence the Ministry found it difficult to distinguish between those office activities that needed a central location and those that did not.

The direct effect of the 1964 ban was more limited than the government had anticipated owing to the large number of developments already in the pipeline. However, the indirect effect of the ban, by imposing an apparent scarcity value on these ongoing or vacant developments and therefore contributing to a general rise in rentals, played directly into the hands of the very people whom it was designed to penalize. And because the ban applied to the whole of London, it had the effect of slowing up short-distance decentralization by restricting the supply of suburban office accommodation.

In response to the ban in London the weight of office development switched to areas in the South East outside the capital. However, before this switch could have much effect the ban was extended in 1966 to the remainder of the South East and West Midlands, East Anglia, and the East Midlands. Nevertheless there were still many very prosperous areas of the country in the South West (e.g. Bristol and Swindon) and the North West (e.g. Cheshire) where office development was never centrally controlled. Owing to the time lag involved in office development, these areas succeeded in catching a number of major decentralizations in the early 1970s (e.g. National Westminster Bank's move to Bristol) because they were the nearest places outside the South East where prime office accommodation was available.

In common with industrial location controls, these physical controls on office development (the 'stick') were complemented by financial inducements for office organizations to move to the development areas (the 'carrot'). But until 1973 the carrot was derisively small compared to that preferred to manufacturing firms. These financial inducements included small building grants which were generally inapplicable since offices prefer to rent accommodation. So although development areas needed office employment, they lacked accommodation to rent. At the level of support available in 1970 Rhodes and Kan estimate that manufacturing industry moving to the development areas was subsidized at least four times as heavily as offices. They quote two examples to support this: (1) a capital-intensive manufacturing plant received a grant of £13·2 million while creating only 2800 jobs, an average of £4100 per job created; (2) an office moving 1000 jobs and building its own office space would receive only £62 800, an average of £625 for each new job created.

The community and individual benefits of office dispersal

This anomaly continued to exist even though it was increasingly acknowledged that office employment could make a particularly significant contribution to regional development problems. In the first place, many manufacturing 'moves' to the development areas were newly established branch plants rather than direct transfers. They therefore did little to relieve pressure in the congested regions. However, in the case of office movement, direct transfers were much more common. More significantly, one component of the multiplier effect associated with an increase in manufacturing jobs in the development areas is likely to be an increase in office jobs which could accrue in congested regions rather than locally within the receiving development area. Movement of high-level office jobs as well as industry could therefore contribute to ensure that benefits were confined to the development areas rather than spreading to other regions. Finally, as Yannopoulos has demonstrated, the local income effects of office development can be significantly greater than that for manufacturing activities (Yannopoulos 1973).

In addition to the public benefits to be gained from office decentralization, it is clear that certain firms gain a number of private benefits irrespective of any financial inducements provided by the community. A detailed study of the costs and benefits of office decentralization has been made by Rhodes and Kan. They found that by far the most important financial saving is that on office rents—especially if account is taken of the fact that decentralized accommodation tends to be new and comparable accommodation in central London would have been more expensive than the offices' existing premises. Another major saving is on staff costs: while there are not great regional variations in wage levels, firms involved in decentralization take the opportunity to reorganize and replace older male staff with lower-paid female staff—for example part-time housewives, recruited in the new location. Not surprisingly the level of this saving is proportional to the number of staff moving with the firm. Staff turnover also tends to be lower in decentralized locations where there is less competition for labour than in Central London.

The principal additional cost incurred by decentralization is that of communications with London and elsewhere. But on average the direct cost of communication (i.e. telephones, postage, stationery, but ignoring travel time) amounts to only 8 per cent of operating costs compared with 73 per cent for staff and 18 per cent for accommodation. However, the indirect costs of travel time and the more important hidden costs resulting from the possible loss of important business contacts were the most important factor preventing many firms from decentralizing. In particular, a move beyond a distance from which it was possible to travel to London and back in one day for a meeting led to greatly increased indirect communications cost. Nevertheless, many firms that had decentralized seem to have solved these problems to their satisfaction. In some instances, decentralization led to an improvement of internal communication between different parts of the organization—for example between a management services department and the production plant it was intend to supervise. Other benefits arose from a changing communications behaviour with regular planned discussions at stated times when someone travelled to London proving more productive than informal and endless chats which took place when individuals were close together in the City.

Having added up all these costs and benefits, Rhodes and Kan concluded that the greatest gains could be made with moves of between 50 and 100 miles from London—that is outside the London labour market but still within easy travel distance of the capital. In general then market forces did not provide any incentive for offices to move to the development areas in preference to other towns in the outer South East, while the government incentives that were available were insufficient to make long-distance movement an economically viable proposition. However, control of office development in the outer South East meant that little office accommodation was available there and consequently many firms moved less than the economically optimum distance or not at all. So it is not surprising that up until 1970 only 1 per cent of all jobs dispersed from London under the auspices of the L.O.B. went to the development areas. In fact Rhodes and Kan's interviews with managers involved in dispersal decisions reveal that they avoided urban areas which contained a high proportion of manufacturing employment. So most dispersals were to small- or medium-sized towns with a particularly desirable residential image. Forty-seven per cent of all moves were in fact confined to the Greater London Area and 78 per cent to places less than 40 miles from Central London. But while they still dominated the picture, L.O.B reported that even the number of short-distance moves began to decline during the late sixties, as the effect of the ban on office development in the South East began to bite.

Because the government exerted a direct control in this field a policy of dispersal of Civil Service jobs was more successful from the point of view of the development areas—that is in terms of the number of jobs moved rather than their level. A total of 50 000 Civil Service jobs were dispersed from London between 1963 and 1972, around 38 per cent of these going to the development areas. Some of the 'moves' were in the form of newly established posts which were being set up outside London, partly because in established divisions key personnel were reluctant to leave the capital. Many of the moves were therefore of low-level clerical jobs which brought only limited benefits to the receiving areas. As in the private sector many of the individual moves involved a limited number of jobs which were widely dispersed over 68 separate locations, an average of 85 jobs per location, with some locations receiving less than 50 posts.

The present situation

In the light of the obvious failure of the existing policy to contribute towards the problem of the development areas, two new measures were introduced in 1973. First, substantial financial inducements were given to office employers to move to the development areas. These were announced on the same day as the government published its proposal for dispersing a substantial number of policy-making Civil Service jobs from London (the Hardman Proposals) (U.K. 1973). The Hardman Report recommended the dispersal of over 31 000 headquarters jobs from the Civil Service in London out of a total of 86 000 jobs considered as possible candidates for relocation. Seventeen per cent of these jobs would go the the development areas and 37 per cent to the intermediate areas.

Although a step in the right direction, these recommendations have been criticized for still failing to do enough for the development areas (e.g. Goddard 1973b). For example, in reviewing only jobs located in Central London, the Hardman study overlooked a large number of potentially mobile government research and development jobs in the South East region outside London. So once again, policy continued to be mesmerized by London. Furthermore, the new policy in the private sector, by relying on the traditional system of financial inducements and physical controls applied over large areas of the country, is unlikely to achieve the selective decentralization of commercial offices of major office centres in the development area which is essential if the community benefits of office policy are to be maximized. The need for such a policy is discussed further in Chapter 6.

The Hardman proposals, nevertheless are significant for regional policy and office location research on a number of grounds. First, one of the main criteria in selecting blocks of work for dispersal was the strength of the communication linkages between various departments in Central London. The methodology developed by the Civil Service Department for this exercise could be particularly relevant to other firms in the private sector considering decentralization. Secondly, in contrast to earlier dispersals in both the private and public sector, some attempt ĩ· was made in the proposal to <u>concentrate relocated employment in a limited number of centres</u>. In addition to the communications advantages to be gained by moving groups of strongly linked departments to a single dispersal location, one of the arguments favouring concentration was the need for an adequate social infrastructure for civil servants. Without this possibility, Civil Servants would have to return to London in order to gain promotion.

As part of the Hardman Report, the Tavistock Institute for Human Relations made a detailed study of the future of the human factor in office decentralization. Before going on to examine the communications factors in more detail in the next chapter we should conclude this examination of office location policy with a very brief look at some of the social implications of office decentralization.

The social implications of office decentralization policies

Research and policy have until recently focused primarily on the economic implications of office decentralization. But such policies also have a wide range of repercussions on the individuals involved in relocation and more particularly on those left behind, repercussions that might not always be desirable from a community point of view (e.g. Burtenshaw 1973, Sidwell 1974). The journey-to-work aspects are perhaps the most obvious (Daniels 1972). The tendency for decentralized offices to be relatively isolated or in quasi-rural locations, a tendency encouraged by decentralization propaganda about working amidst the green fields, has meant that non-car-owners can have considerable problems of access to employment opportunities 'out of town'. In addition problems arise for the dependents of those moving with their jobs, especially if they are also economically active. Unless the decentralization is to a large and diversified labour market, some depends may be unemployed for a long time or take a job below their qualifications. Such underuse of manpower resources is something the nation in general and the hard-pressed London labour market in particular can ill afford.

Recent attention has therefore been focused on the labour market implications for London of an active policy of office decentralization. The evidence reported already (p. 39) that <u>firms use the opportunity of decentralization to get rid of unwanted older male employees</u> could have a number of long-term repercussions for the capital. The relative decline of clerical employment opportunities in Central London coupled with an increase in high-level jobs whose employees have a choice of commuting from outside London or living near their work could contribute to serious problems of <u>social polarization in the Inner City</u> (Eversley 1973).

Such problems are already far more serious in American cities. Here the suburbanization of office employment, for example to freeway interchanges, has threatened to undermine the economic base of the central city. A defensive investment to protect the economic interest of city centres has resulted (Manners 1973). The Regional Plan Association of New York concludes that such investment is also essential on social grounds. They argue that policy should aim to reinforce the central business district and especially office centres in the inner city. Widespread dispersal of office development, although economically easier and most feasible in the short run, could be both economically and socially disastrous in the long run (Armstrong and Pushkarev 1973).

The Greater London Council is aware of such issues and has modified its attitude towards office decentralization accordingly. By the early 1960s many local authorities in the London area had already become less enamoured of the idea of office decentralization, particularly in view of the unexpected planning headaches such schemes had produced, especially in the form of traffic congestion. Public transport can only be utilized if office development is concentrated into a limited number of centres, but this requires a substantial investment in infrastructure as the experience of Croydon has clearly pointed out. So current policy favours the development of major office centres in inner urban as well as suburban locations, the former especially to diversify the range of job opportunities in the inner city (G.L.C. 1973). Selective restriction on office activities remains the keynote in central London, although the means by which such a selective policy can be operated are far from clear (G.L.C. 1970, Goddard 1970a).

5 The communication factors in office decentralization

Introduction

In Chapter 4 we have seen that decentralization has been the prime objective of office location policy. One of the most important constraining factors in firms' decisions about decentralization is the strong belief that vital personal contacts with clients, suppliers, and advisers—in fact the pool of information that can readily be tapped in the city centre— would be lost if the firm were to move too far away. Such fears become increasingly significant as the amount of routine work (i.e. that involving little communication with other firms) available for decentralization declines. And even in the case of routine work there may be problems of communication with head office.

The words 'belief' and 'fears' are used advisedly because there is little hard evidence available to firms on the likely impact of relocation on their communication patterns. Whilst stressing the importance of communications factors, very few office organizations have any detailed knowledge about their existing contact patterns. The sort of data collected by contact diaries that were used to analyse aggregate information flows in Central London in Chapter 3 are an essential prerequisite for individual firms which wish to estimate the likely effect of decentralization on their business communications. The contact data may be used to indicate which departments or functions have weak linkages with the city centre and are therefore likely candidates for relocation. The approach would be much the same as that adopted at the more aggregate level in Chapter 3 in identifying business sectors weakly integrated into the Central London contact network. Data on the volume of communication between blocks of work in the Civil Service, for example, have already provided an important component in a decision-making model designed to suggest appropriate decentralization patterns for this work (Elton *et al.* 1970; Goddard 1971; U.K. 1973). Similar material has been used in Sweden as a basis for selecting government agencies for dispersal from Stockholm (Thorngren 1973).

However, even with this type of information it is still extremely difficult to predict exactly what will happen to existing contacts if a particular office relocates. There are a number of possibilities. Some contacts will be maintained with the old location but will involve longer journeys or the increased use of existing or novel forms of telecommunication. In the long run, however, some former contacts will no longer occur or will be replaced by new links in the decentralized location. For example, a local accountant in a new location may provide services originally supplied by a London firm.

Whatever happens in detail, we can be sure that relocation will involve change in communications behaviour that will have more far-reaching consequences than the direct communication costs such as telephone bills, fares, and even travel time. This is because the contact patterns both with other firms and other parts of the organization located elsewhere ultimately define the role of a particular office within an organization. New patterns of contact—that is who has talked to whom, about what, and how often—will mean that the office in a new location is playing a different role from previously. For example, frequent, short, and unarranged meetings that existed in the city centre may be replaced by pre-planned long discussions in the new location; given the nature of interpersonal contacts it is likely that these meetings will have a different significance.

These effects of relocation on office communication may be broadly summarized under three headings: (1) transferability; (2) substitutability; (3) functional change. The first heading refers to the possibility of transferring city centre contacts to the new locality; the second to the possibility of transferring city centre contacts that have not been replaced locally to telecommunications; the third heading is most fundamental in the sense that contact transfers and substitutability are both a consequence of the way the functions of the organization change as a result of decentralization.

While it can be difficult to predict exactly the changes in communication behaviour that will result from relocation of a particular office, the experience of firms that have already moved can provide an important guide to the likely effects, especially if these contact patterns are compared with those of similar firms in the old location. Furthermore, by contrasting firms in the old location prior to the move with those that have rejected relocation explicitly on communication grounds, it should be possible to assess the role of the communications factor in office location decisions. Such a study has recently been completed for the Location of Offices Bureau in which the communications behaviour of firms that have moved different distances from Central London were compared to firms who have remained (Goddard and Morris 1975).

Functional differences between city centre and decentralized offices

Variations in the amount and type of contact generated by different offices provide an important guide as to their function within an organization and can help identify units which are potential candidates for decentralization. If we compare the number of telephone and meeting contacts recorded by individuals in a small sample of firms about to decentralize (the movers) with those that have rejected decentralization specifically on communication grounds (the non-movers) we see that the former have 58 per cent fewer external calls and 55 per cent fewer external meetings (an average of 6·2 calls and 1·3 meetings per week compared with 19·2 calls and 3·0 meetings per week for the non-movers). Offices that have made a conscious decision to remain in the city centre appear to have more contact than the average while those selected for dispersal have much less contact (Table 5.1). Nevertheless, decentralized offices still have 5 per cent fewer external calls and 25 per cent fewer meetings than other firms in Central London prior to moving, suggesting a possible loss of some contacts. Internal meetings on the other hand are 50 per cent more numerous in decentralized offices, suggesting that more time is devoted to internal matters.

TABLE 5.1
Variations in contact intensity

| | Meetings per respondent | | Telephone calls per respondent | |
	External	*Internal*	*External*	*Internal*
Average for Central London	2·2	N/A	7·7	N/A
Central London 'movers'	0·6	0·2	3·7	5·5
Central London 'non-movers'	1·6	0·8	9·0	5·3
Decentralized offices	0·6	0·4	1·0	4·9

Note: Figures are average number of contacts recorded per respondent in a three day period.   N/A = not available.
Source: Goddard and Morris (1975).

Differences in the amount of contact are partly a reflection of the characteristics of the contacts themselves. The higher intensity of contacts recorded by non-movers compared with movers and by Central London offices compared with decentralized offices can largely be attributed to a much higher frequency of contact. For example, 22 per cent of the external calls of non-movers occur on a daily basis compared with only 6 per cent for movers and 8 per cent for decentralized offices. Similarly, only 6 per cent of the external meetings of the decentralized offices are daily contacts compared with 24 per cent for Central London offices as a whole. Because of their close connection with contact frequency, a wide range of other differences in the characteristics of contacts follow from this basic distinction. Frequent contacts tend to be shorter, unarranged or arranged only the day before, and to involve a limited number of familiar people in rather specific discussions. A short contact is therefore more likely to involve simply giving or receiving information rather than a wide-ranging exchange. Frequent short contacts therefore tend to fulfil a different function than long pre-planned meetings.

The combined differences in these characteristics can be summarized in a multivariate classification of contacts using latent profile analysis, which aims at identifying those which are of the orientation, planning, and programmed variety (see pp. 19—20 for a discussion of this conceptual classification). It will be recalled that orientation relations tend to occur in large pre-planned meetings involving wide-ranging talks between people coming into contact for the first time. Planning relations on the other hand tend to involve more limited numbers of familiar individuals in intensive rather than extensive discussions; being familiar, individuals can make greater use of the telephone than in orientation relations. Programmed contacts also involve familiar people who are in frequent contact but about very routine matters. Fig. 5.1 describes such a classification of external contacts for Central London offices.

Although all three types of contact may be identified in most organizations in different locations, the relative importance of each type differs significantly. Not only do 'movers' have fewer external contacts but the

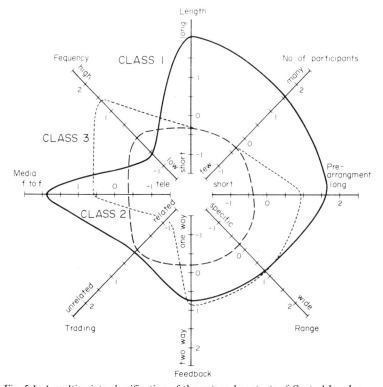

Fig. 5.1. A multivariate classification of the external contacts of Central London offices. The axes are in standardized units with zero equal to the average for each variable (from Goddard 1973a).

these are most likely to be of the programmed variety (Table 5.2), indicating that these particular offices play a rather limited role within their organizations. This is partly a reflection of the fact that relatively few contacts are with the orientation environment of the city centre. So these offices are clearly at odds with their local environment, having the communication characteristics of offices that have already decentralized rather than those of other offices in the city centre. Decentralized offices also have fewer orientation contacts than offices in Central London as a whole. Conversely, firms that have rejected decentralization have proportionally more orientation contacts than other firms in Central London

TABLE 5.2
The relative importance of contacts of different type

| | Orientation | | Planning | | Programmed | |
	Ext. %	Int. %	Ext. %	Int. %	Ext. %	Int. %
Average for Central London	14·5	N/A	4·2	N/A	81·2	N/A
Central London 'movers'	14·8	6·5	3·5	1·1	81·7	75·8
Central London 'non-movers'	24·1	6·9	8·5	4·2	67·4	60·9
Decentralized offices	10·3	7·3	1·1	17·7	88·6	74·9

Note: N/A = not available
Source: Goddard and Morris (1975).

The geographical distribiton of contacts of offices in different locational situations

We have suggested that the lower level of orientation contacts of offices about to decentralize is due to the fact that as well as having fewer contacts over all, these offices have less connection with other firms in Central London compared with other places (Table 5.3 confirms this). However, offices that have already decentralized have even fewer contacts with Central London. On average individuals in Central London have 58 per cent of their external telephone calls with other people in the centre compared with 38 per cent for those that have moved up to 60 miles and 14 per cent for those moving over 60 miles. Conversely, the number of contacts with places outside the South-East region increases with distance moved. The evidence of the distribution of the contacts of the movers suggests that some of these contacts may have been established before the relocation. Nevertheless some of these must be 'new' contacts established subsequent to the move.

The sharp decline of contacts with Central London for moves of over 60 miles can be related to the geography of contact opportunities and

TABLE 5.3

The geographical distribution of external contacts

Telephone

	A		B		C		D		E	
	No	%	No	%	No	%	No	%	No	%
Central London	3055	58	326	38	37	14	50	42	174	63
Greater London	1002	19	214	25	30	11	35	30	27	10
South East	421	8	161	19	66	25	11	9	26	9
Rest of UK	632	12	148	17	133	50	20	17	49	18
Overseas	156	3	14	2	–	–	2	2	–	–
TOTAL	5266		863		266		118		276	

Meeting

	A		B		C		D		E	
Central London	1250	64	87	32	42	22	12	50	80	79
Greater London	293	15	76	28	23	12	5	21	8	8
South East	98	5	68	24	68	35	5	21	6	6
Rest of UK	176	9	39	14	58	30	1	4	7	7
Overseas	137	7	6	2	2	1	1	4	–	–
TOTAL	1954		276		193		24		101	

A   Central London Survey 1970.
B   Survey of decentralized offices: firms which had moved up to 60 miles from London.
C   Survey of decentralized offices: firms which had moved to beyond 60 miles from London.
D   Central London firms which had decided to decentralize.
E   Central London firms which had decided to remain in Central London.

Source: Goddard and Morris (1975).

the pattern of decentralization. In spite of the large amount of office employment in the South East region outside London, much of this is extremely dispersed; consequently the possibilities of establishing local contacts with the immediate environment are limited. London therefore exerts a strong shadow effect. However, over 60 miles from London, larger office centres can be found which can provide realistic contact alternatives to London.

Differences in the geographical distribution of contacts for short- and long-distance movers are reflected in average journey times to meetings; firms moving a long way from London have on average *shorter* journeys to business meetings than firms moving less far. For example, 33 per cent of business journeys of firms moving over 80 miles last less than 30 minutes, compared with an average of 10 per cent for firms moving between 20 and 80 miles. Nevertheless, the amount of time spent on business travel by decentralized offices is obviously much greater than that spent by offices in Central London or long-established offices elsewhere (compare with Chapter 2, p. 16), reflecting the fact that many of these firms have not yet completely adjusted to the contact opportunities of their local environment and also possibly a mistaken choice of isolated suburban rather than city-centre sites in the new locations.

Relocation as a response to changing contact needs

The evidence of these data suggests that offices that have already decentralized or have decided to move in the near future have made rational location decisions at least with respect to communications factors. In the main it is routine or programmed functions that have been relocated.

These relocation decisions should be seen in the context of the continually evolving structure of the office organization. New activities within either an established company or an independent firm may need a large number of external links; however, at a later stage in the development of the organization, routines may become more standardized and the dependence on the local environment less significant. In the case of a head office function within a manufacturing firm, for example, the weight of contact needs over time may change from external relations with the decision-making functions of other firms in the city centre to internal connections to production units located elsewhere in the country. Policy decisions may be made, for example with respect to purchasing, which profoundly influence the location of potential contact sources—away from London to a particular region of the country. Although location is not a cause of such changes, the decisions themselves may create both the need and the opportunity for new locational arrangements. At any one point in time this need will be reflected in the pattern of interaction between the office and its external and internal environment. The important point is that relocation should bring the organization more into line with its current contact needs. It should therefore be used as a tool to support specific management objectives. The fact that decentralized offices have fewer high-level contacts, especially with Central London, is of significance only if the relocated office is expected to perform an orientation function. If, however, the objective is to improve internal communications, a decline in external contacts will be a positive benefit. If both objectives need to be met and it is not possible to split the organization geographically, then telecommunications may be used to reconcile the conflicting location pulls and used as a substitute for business travel.

Telecommunications and office decentralization

We have already noted that individuals in decentralized offices spend more time in business travel than in the case for city centre offices or offices generally (p. 48). Can telecommunications act as a substitute for some of these business journeys? We may assess the potential for greater use of telecommunications in decentralized offices by comparing the features of contacts recorded there with the capabilities of various telecommunication systems.

At present most people have a choice between a face-to-face meeting and a telephone call. The conventional telephone obviously imposes severe constraints on interpersonal communications—for example only two people can take part, documents cannot be shown or visual reactions assessed. However, recent developments in telecommunications technology have overcome many of these problems. In our survey of contacts in decentralized offices we find that the most important reason for a person having a meeting rather than using a telephone is the 'need to consult,   i exchange or sign documents'. Facsimile transmission devices can now be linked to telephones which can overcome this difficulty. The second   ii most important reason is 'the need for a group to take part'. Conference calls can now be arrange linking a number of individuals in different locations. However, these have the disadvantage that is is difficult to identify individual speakers. This difficulty can be overcome by the use of remote meeting tables linked by a conventional telephone line where each 'absent' participant is represented by a loudspeaker.

Both group audio and document transmission facilities are relatively cheap as they are 'narrow band' systems requiring a limited number of telephone lines. The third most important reason for persons in decentralized offices preferring meetings is 'the need to gather background   iii information'. This type of reason refers to informal relations that can occur in a meeting but which would require a video channel if telecommunications were to be a suitable alternative. Video communication systems like the Post Office's Confravision require expensive 'broad band' links (up to 100 telephone lines or their equivalent). Special studios are needed and extra costs may be involved in travel to the studios. In addition to the cost involved the formalization of meetings that conference video systems require may effectively rule out the establishment of new informal relations that are essential if the contact is to perform an orientation function. So the potential for conference video systems may be limited at present. At the same time video-phones work in the area of two-person communication where the ordinary telephone is already satisfactory.

However, not all meetings are of the orientation variety; in fact in decentralized offices around a quarter are of a programmed character— that is giving or receiving of information to and from someone with whom the participant is familiar. These types of exchange can be dealt with by the conventional telephone so we here have an indication of a less than efficient use of some face-to-face meetings. Planning contacts are also between familiar individuals but it is more likely that the discussion will require two-way exchanges of information and also the showing of documents. The familiarity of the participants places these contacts in a category where telecommunications can be used, and this certainly seems to be the case when decentralization occurs; all external planning contacts are by telephone in decentralized locations compared with only 50 per cent in central London. So planning functions are probably good candidates for decentralization.

It would be reasonable to expect that the potential for substituting telecommunications for face-to-face meetings increases as the geograph separation of the participants in a potential contact increases. However as far as decentralized offices are concerned, it should be remembered that firms moving beyond the South East region tend to go to larger office centres where there are greater opportunities for establishing loc contacts and therefore reducing the average length of business journeys Also, contacts involving longer journeys tend to be at a much higher level and, therefore, have characteristics which make substitution difficult. So the greatest potential for substitution is with short-distance contacts, contacts which are the exception rather than the rule in the case of decentralized offices.

These findings, based on the characteristics of contacts that have actually occurred, are reinforced by considerations of the relative cost of different types of telecommunication systems, including the value given to the businessman's time. A simple equation of this relationship has been suggested by Elton and Pye (1973). Applying these equations to the Communications Studies Group's contact data shows that narro band systems (4 times the cost of a conventional telephone call) are always cheaper than travel if the studio is 'in house', and cheaper if time is valued at twice the individual's salary when travel to a studio is required. Time has to be valued very highly before broad-band systems become economic. However, a much larger proportion of meetings will be economical by telecommunications if the studio facilities are in hou a situation which is most likely to apply to the internal contacts be twee dispersed parts of large organizations. Because new facilities will diffuse only slowly through the telecommunications systems it is most likely that different parts of the same organization will be linked with comparable equipment before different organizations. Telecommunications are therefore likely to encourage further partial dispersal of office functions from capital cities, while top-level functions remain firmly in the centre.

Conclusion

We have discussed the possibility of telecommunications acting as a substitute for business travel and therefore favouring greater office decentralization. We conclude this chapter with a cautionary note. The word 'substitute' suggests that telecommunications is either as good as or a poor alternative to the face-to-face meeting. However, in a number of instances the use of telecommunications may be more effective than the meeting not only in terms of immediate time-saving but also in allowing greater flexibility in the scheduling of other activities. The introduction of advanced telecommunication facilities in a decentralize office may help make the meetings that have to take place more effective by permitting essential preliminary discussions: telecommunication may therefore generate as many new contacts as it substitutes for. Elton, therefore, suggests that telecommunications should be seen as *enabling* new patterns of contact behaviour to develop on decentralization rather than simply as a straight substitution for old contacts previously held face-to-face in the city centre (Elton 1974). Telecommunications therefore are another factor that can contribute to changes in contact behaviour on relocation.

6 Current research and the reformulation of office location policy

The traditional concern of office location policy has been the dispersal of office employment from the centres of large cities with little attention being paid to where this employment is relocated. The outstanding conclusions of much of the research that we have reviewed is that this office dispersal needs to be concentrated into a limited number of major office centres with an adequate economic, social, and communications infrastructure if the individual and community benefits are to be maximized and undesirable side-effects minimized. In these concluding pages we shall detail how research has suggested the need for such a revision of *public policy*. Since this policy can only be effected through the location of decisions of individual organizations, we shall principally examine how research can be used to inform such decisions.

Before deciding on a relocation an individual organization clearly needs to take account of its existing and future communications requirements. A communications survey of existing internal (inter-departmental) and external (inter-firm) contacts can suggest a relocation stragegy which supports management objectives. Our findings that individuals communicate in different ways in different places suggest that relocation can be used as a positive tool in management; for example it can be used to bring together departments which need to communicate more with each other and perhaps less with other firms; to improve linkages with other firms that are located elsewhere, perhaps in newly emerging spheres of interest for the organizations; to encourage the devolution of some functions to lower levels in the organization thereby creating space and time in a city centre office for decision-making activities.

The important point is that some relocation strategies may be more appropriate than others for achieving particular management objectives. For example short-distance relocation to a small office centre will not encourage the establishment of new local linkages which might be an essential component of an administrative decentralization strategy. It is therefore necessary to distinguish between the *dispersal* of offices—which is a purely geographical concept—and *decentralization* which is also a functional concept which geographical separation may encourage. If, however, there is a need to release time for essential internal matters then movement to a minor office centre not far from the capital may be a good alternative for planning or research and development functions.

The success or otherwise of the relocation will need to be monitored by regular communications surveys or 'audits'. These data may suggest additional changes in the formal organizational structure or new telecommunications devices that are needed in order to derive the maximum benefits from the new location. In addition to evaluating the relocation as such, the audits may indicate potential future problems that may have to be dealt with by further organizational/locational adjustments. For example the audits may indicate 'blind spots' in external contact networks (e.g. sectors of the environment not covered by any part of the organization) or a failure to link up external and internal networks so that outside information is not channelled to the appropriate parts of the organization.

Here as elsewhere in this book emphasis is placed upon the role of information flows in the development of organizations. Little attention has been paid to the direct costs of communications. The ease with which contact networks can adjust to new organizational and locational situations means that attempts to formally determine the communications costs and benefits of particular location strategies are of limited validity. Because of the large area of uncertainty and the speed with which changes can occur, a process of monitoring a selected strategy coupled with appropriate adjustments in that strategy is probably more appropriate than a 'one shot' cost-benefit analysis. Decentralization should therefore be seen not solely as a short-run economic decision with respect to such factors as rents, labour costs, and telephone bills, but as part of a process by which organizations can adapt to changing environmental conditions. So, although a relatively short move to a small office centre may suit present-day contact requirements and also be the most economical solution on a number of other cost grounds, only a large office centre can offer the number and variety of local contact opportunities that can sustain an office organization when external conditions change.

So a public policy of *concentrated decentralization* may also bring long-run benefits to individual firms. For example within such centres there will be possibilities of using narrow-band telecommunications for intra-urban contact and public studios for inter-city broad-band telecommunications: it is unlikely that a large number of dispersed locations will be equipped with such facilities at least in the short run. The public benefits of such a pattern are numerous. On the economic side there is the possibility of the development of complexes of interrelated office functions which can provide external economies for the constituent activities but which act as a stimulus for growth and change in the surrounding region. So although the growth centre based on a propulsive industry may not be a particularly useful proposition in terms of material linkages such a centre could have very real meaning in terms of office location and associated information flows. On the social side there are the benefits to be gained by a labour market with a diversified occupational structure and possibilities for the use of public transport.

Unless present-day policies are modified and individual office relocation decisions co-ordinated, an opportunity for creating such centres may be lost. Concentrated decentralization clearly needs some new instruments to bring about the detailed steering of economic activities that this policy implies. The existing blanket controls on physical development and financial incentives applied over equally wide areas of the country are very blunt policy instruments. The subtle ways in which firms can adapt to environmental change through administrative reorganization, which may include alterations in the division of office functions between locations, suggest that the location process as such is extremely difficult to control from the point of view of regional policy.

Because the process of environmental adaption is heavily sustained by information channelled through established networks, contact patterns are a key element in the process of change *and* also control. Firms frequently make sub-optimal decisions based on a failure to appreciate fully the constraints on information flows imposed by their own organizational structure. Communications audits administered by a public body could be a very powerful tool in regional policy by highlighting for firms the opportunities of alternative locational/organizational arrangements, especially the advantages to be gained through different but complementary offices locating in similar areas. Communications surveys could also reveal the possibility of linking up complementary functions in different offices in nearby regions perhaps in order to complete an office complex. In addition to encouraging the relocation of specific office functions to specific places policy would also need to recognize the importance of new office activities that are indigenous to the area in question.

This approach implies a much greater involvement of government in a collaborative way in the long-run strategic planning decisions of office organizations rather than a crude carrot and stick approach applied to the geographical environment and not to the decision-making units the policy is aimed at. Nevertheless this is not to deny the need for spatial policies which designate office growth centres and thereby provide a basis for linking urban and regional policy and co-ordinating these policies with investment in passenger transport and telecommunications. Unless far-reaching changes in government policy which take account of the influence of contact possibilities on regional development are implemented, the existing spiral of over-concentration will continue. Indeed if investment in communications infrastructure such as conference video facilities and advanced passenger trains is uncoordinated with location policy, it is only likely to increase regional differentials in contact opportunities and ultimately in economic and social development.

Select bibliography

Chapter One

Daniels, P. W. (1975) *Offices: An Urban Regional Study,* Bell, London. A comprehensive review of office development research covering the genesis of the office function, the growth of office employment, the supply and demand for office floorspace, as well as much of the material on interregional and intra-urban office location only touched upon in this book.

Cowan, P., *et al.* (1969) *The Office: A Facet of Urban Growth,* Heinemann, London. The first major British research study of office location and development concentrating particularly on London.

Armstrong, R. A. and Pushkarev, B. (1973) *The Office Industry: Patterns of Growth and Location,* M.I.T. Press, Cambridge, Mass. A comprehensive statistical compendium of American experience.

Chapter Two

Törnqvist, G. (1970) *Contact Systems and Regional Development,* Lund Studies in Geography (B) No. 35. An introduction to the relationship between information flows and the location of office occupations.

Chapter Three

Goddard, J. B. (1973a) *Office Linkages and Location: a Study of Communications and Spatial Patterns in Central London,* Pergamon Press, Oxford. Contains most of the empirical material on which Chapter 3 and parts of Chapter 5 are based.

Chapter Four

Rhodes, J. and Kan, A. (1972) *Office Dispersal and Regional Policy,* Occasional Paper No. 30, Department of Applied Economics, University of Cambridge, Cambridge University Press, Cambridge. A critical evaluation of office location policy up to 1972 which pointed the way to the new measures introduced in 1973.

Chapter Five

Goddard, J. B. and Morris, D. M. (1975) *The Communications Factor in Office Decentralization,* Pergamon Press, Oxford. The survey of office communications in decentralized locations which was a follow-up to that in Central London described under Chapter 3.

References

Aguilar, F. J. (1967) *Scanning the Business Environment,* Macmillan, New York.

Armstrong, R. A. and Pushkarev, B. (1973) *The Office Industry: Patterns of Growth and Location,* MIT Press, Cambridge, Mass.

Berry, B. J. L. (1966) *Commodity Flows and the Spatial Structure of the Indian Economy,* Research Paper no. 111, Dept. of Geography, Univ. of Chicago, Ill.

— (1972) 'Hierarchical Diffusion: the Basis of Developmental Filtering and Spread in a System of Growth Centres', in Hansen, M. M. (ed.), *Growth Centres in Regional Economic Development,* Free Press, New York.

Brams, S. J. (1966) 'Transaction Flows in the International System', *American Political Science Review,* 60, 880–98.

Britton, J. (1974) 'Environmental Adaption of Industrial Plants: Service Linkages, Locational Environment and Organization', in Hamilton, F. E. I. (ed.), *Spatial Perspectives on Industrial Organization and Decision Making,* Wiley, London.

Burrow, M. (1973) 'Office employment and the regional problem', *Regional Studies,* 7, 17–31.

Burtenshaw, D. (1973) 'Relocation Wives', *New Society,* 21 June 1973.

Buswell, R. J. and Lewis, E. W. (1970) 'The Geographical Distribution of Industrial Research Activity in the U.K.', *Regional Studies,* 4, 297–306.

Connell, S. (1973) *The 1973 Office Communications Survey,* Communications Studies Group, London (P/74067/CN).

Cowan, P., *et al.* (1969) *The Office: A Facet of Urban Growth,* Heinemann, Lond.

Daniels, P. (1972) 'Transport Changes Generated by Decentralized Offices', *Regional Studies,* 6, 273–289.

Dill, W. R. (1962) 'The Impact of Environment on Organizational Development', in Mailick, S. and van Ness, E. H. (eds.), *Concepts and Issues in Administrative Behaviour,* Prentice Hall, Englewood Cliffs, N. J.

Dunning, J. H. and Morgan, E. V. (1971) *An Economic Study of the City of London,* Allen and Unwin, London.

EFTA (1973) *National Settlement Strategies: a Framework for Regional Development,* Geneva.

Elton, M., *et al.* (1970) *An approach to the Location of Government,* Institute of Management Science, London (mimeo).

Elton, M., and Pye, R. (1973) *Travel or Comminicate? The Comparative Costs,* Communications Studies Group, London (P/73166/EC).

Elton, M. (1974) 'The Use of Communications Surveys to Assess the Scope for Advanced Person to Person Telecommunications', Paper presented at a seminar on Organizational Communications, International Institute of Management, Berlin (mimeo).

Engström, M. G. (1970) *Regional arbetsfördelning,* Gleerup, Lund. (English summary: The regional division of labour: new trends in the geographical organization of employment in Sweden.)

Eversley, D. C. (1973) 'Rising Costs and Static Incomes: some Economic Consequences of Regional Planning in London', in G. C. Cameron and L. Wingon (eds.), *Cities, Regions and Public Policy,* Oliver and Boyd, Edinburgh.

G.L.C. (1970) *Greater London Development Plan Statement,* G.L.C., London.

— (1973) *London: the Future and You. Population and Employment,* G.L.C., London.

Goddard, J. B. (1966) 'The Internal Structure of London's Central Area', in M. van Hulten (ed.), *Urban Core and Inner City,* Brill, Leiden.

— (1967) 'Changing Office Location Patterns in Central London', *Urban Studies,* 4, 276–85. Longmans, Harlow.

— (1970a) 'Greater London Development Plan: Central London, a Key to Strategic Planning', *Area,* 3, 52–5.

References 59

Goddard, J. B. (1970b) 'Functional Regions within the City Centre: a Study by
   Factor Analysis of Taxi Flows in Central London, *Transactions and Papers,
   Institute of British Geographers*, **49**, 161–82.
– (1971) 'Office Communications and Office Location: a Review of Current
   Research', *Regional Studies*, pp. 263–280.
– (1973a) *Office Linkages and Location*, Progress in Planning (1), Pergamon Press,
   Oxford.
– (1973b) 'Civil Service for the Regions', *Town and Country Planning*.
– and Morris, D. M. (1975) *The Communications Factor in Office Decentralization*,
   Mimograph, London School of Economics.
Gottman, J. (1970) 'Urban Centrality and the Inter-weaving of Quaternary Functions',
   Ekistics, **29**, 322–31.
Hall, P. (1971) 'The Spatial Structure of Metropolitan England and Wales', in
   M. Chisholm and G. Manners (eds.), *Spatial Policy Problems of the British
   Economy*, Cambridge University Press, Cambridge.
Hall, P. K. (1972) 'Movement of Offices from Central London', *Regional Studies*,
   6, 385–392.
Hedberg, B. (1970) *Kontaktsystem Inom Svenskt Navingsliv*, Gleerups, Lund.
   (English summary: Contact systems in the Swedish Economy: a study of the
   external personal contacts of organizations.)
Jantsch (1967) *Technological Forecasting in Perspective*, O.E.C.D., Paris.
Manners, G. (1973) *The Office in the Metropolis: An Opportunity for Shaping
   Metropolitan America*, Working Paper No. 22, Joint Center for Urban Studies
   of the Massachusetts Institute of Technology and Harvard University.
Marriott, O. (1967) *The Property Boom*, Hamish Hamilton, London.
Meir, R. L. (1962) *A Communications Theory of Urban Growth*, MIT Press,
   Cambridge, Mass.
Morgan, W. T. W. (1961) 'A Functional Approach to the Study of Office
   Distributions' *Tijdschrift voor Economische en Sociale Geographie*, **52**, 207–10.
Parsons, G. (1972) 'The Giant Manufacturing Corporations and Balanced Regional
   Growth in Britain', *Area*, **4**, 99–103.
Pred, A. (1973) 'The Growth and Development of Systems of Cities in Advanced
   Economies', in Pred, and Törnqvist (1973).
– and Törqvist, G. (1973) *System of Cities and Information Flows*, Lund Studies
   in Geography (B), No. 38, Gleerup, Lund.
Rannels, J. (1956) *The Core of the City*, University of Columbia Press, New York.
Rhodes, J. and Kan, A. (1971) *Office Dispersal and Regional Policy*, Department
   of Applied Economics, Cambridge.
Sahlberg, B. (1970) *Interregionala Kontakmönster*, Gleerup, Lund. (English
   summary: Interregional Contact Flows.)
Savage, R. and Deutsch, K. W. (1960) 'A Statistical Model of the Gross Analysis of
   Transaction Flows', *Econometrica*, **28**, 551–72.
Sidwell, E. (1974) *The Problems for Employees in Office Dispersal: a Methodology*,
   Discussion Paper No. 46, London School of Economics, Graduate Geography
   Department.
Steed, G. P. F. (1971) 'Changing Processes of Corporate Environment Relations',
   Area, **3**, 207–11.
Thorngren, B. (1967) 'Regional Economic Interaction and Flows of Information',
   in *Proceedings of the Second Poland-Norden Regional Science Seminar*,
   Committee for Space Economy and Regional Planning of the Polish Academy
   of Sciences, PWN, Warsaw.
– (1968) 'External Economies and the Urban Core' in M. Van Hulten (ed.),
   Urban Core and Inner City, Brill, Leiden.
– (1970) 'How do Contact Systems Affect Regional Development?', *Environment
   and Planning*, **2**, 409–27.
– (1973) 'Swedish office dispersal', in Bannon, M. (ed.), *Office Location and
   Regional Development*, An Foras Forbartha, Dublin.
Törnqvist, G. (1970) *Contact Systems and Regional Development*, Lund Studies
   in Geography (B) No. 35.
– (1973) 'Contact Requirements and Travel Facilities: Contact Models of Sweden
   and Regional Development Alternatives in the future', in Pred and Törnqvist 1973.

U.K. (1973) *The Dispersal of Government Work from London* (The Hardman Report), H.M.S.O., Cmnd. 5322.

Watts, H. D. (1972) 'Giant Manufacturing Corporations: Further Observations on Regional Growth and Large Corporations', *Area,* 4, p. 269.

Wärneryd, O. (1968) *Interdependence in Urban Systems,* Regionkonsult Aktiebolo Gothenburg.

Webber, M. N. (1964) 'The Urban Place and non-Place Urban Realm', in D. L. Fol et al. (eds.), *Explorations into Urban Instructure,* University of Pennsylvania Press, Philadelphia.

Westaway, E. J. (1974a) 'Contact Potentials and the Occupational Structure of the British Urban System 1961–66: an Empircal Study', *Regional Studies,* 8, 57–73.

– (1974b) 'The Spatial Hierarchy of Business Organizations and its Implications for the British Urban System', *Regional Studies,* 8, pp. 145–155.

Yannopoulos, G. (1973) 'The Local Income effect of Office Relocation', *Regional Studies,* 7, pp. 33–46.